The Biteback Dictionary of

HUMOROUS

POLITICAL

QUOTATIONS

—— *Fred Metcalf* ——

Biteback Publishing

First published in Great Britain in 2012 by
Biteback Publishing Ltd
Westminster Tower
3 Albert Embankment
London SE1 7SP
Copyright © Fred Metcalf 2012

ISBN 978-1-84954-224-1

10 9 8 7 6 5 4 3 2 1

A CIP catalogue record for this book is available from the British Library.

Set in Sabon

Printed and bound in Great Britain by
CPI Group (UK) Ltd, Croydon CR0 4YY

CONTENTS

Introduction   v

A: Agriculture to Axioms and Advice   1
B: Baldwin, Stanley to Business   18
C: Cameron, David to Cuba   43
D: Death Penalty to Drugs   80
E: Economics and Economists to European Union   100
F: Fanaticism to Free Speech   128
G: Germany and the Germans to Government   140
H: Harding, Warren G. to House of Lords   148
I: Immigration to Ireland and the Irish   161
J: Johnson, Boris to Justice   176
K: Kennedy, John F.   180
L: Labour Party to Local Government   182
M: MacDonald, Ramsay to Multiculturalism   208
N: Nationalism to Nuclear Weapons   217
O: Obama, Barack to Opposition   225
P: Palin, Sarah to Protest   232
Q: Quayle, Dan   269
R: Race to Royalty   270
S: Science to Stock Market   289
T: Taxation to Tyrants   309
V: Vice Presidency to Voting   322
W: Wales and the Welsh to Work   326

INTRODUCTION

One of the most famous orations in American political history is the 'Cross of Gold' speech delivered on 9 July 1896 by William Jennings Bryan at the Democratic National Convention in Chicago.

According to reports at the time, his dramatic speaking style – applied to the arcane subject of the money supply – roused the crowd to such a frenzy that, according to the *Washington Post*, 'Bedlam broke loose and delirium reigned supreme.'

It's said that it took more than twenty-five minutes to restore order.

The speech helped catapult Bryan to the Democratic Party's nomination for President. As the humorous commentator Will Rogers put it, 'He can take a batch of words and scramble them together and leaven them properly with a hunk of oratory and knock the White House doorknob right out of a candidate's hand.'

Contesting the election, Bryan delivered his 'Cross of Gold' speech 500 times across America in the course of a year.

And yet he still lost – to William McKinley, who became the 25th President of the United States.

Of course, it's easy to be wise in hindsight, but having examined the manuscript of the speech in detail, I think I've identified his key problem – no humour.

To sum up: no jokes, no quotes, no droll bons mots.

Let's face it, any gag writer worth his salt could have provided Bryan with ten good money-supply gags in thirty minutes. The problem was that no one had yet assumed the role of joke writer in 1896. But for the absence of a few topical one-liners in Bryan's speech, McKinley would have been in no position later to annex Hawaii, declare war on Spain or, from a more personal point of view, get shot by an assassin in 1901.

／It was Victor Hugo who almost said, 'There is nothing more powerful than a quote whose time has come.'

It may not be their first coming for the quotations in this book, but this is the first time they have been brought together en masse for the purpose of amusing and enlightening, while at the same time, of course, comforting the afflicted and afflicting the comfortable – not to say changing minds, including your own.

The prime purpose of this book is, of course, to amuse.

It is for those who appreciate the restorative power of a good joke or an amusing quotation; an invaluable collection, perfect for writers and orators needing an injection of humour into stolid words, as well as for the politician floundering with the economy or the economist languishing in politics.

Having a copy of this book is like having a joke writer in your pocket. (Or are you just tickled to see me?) With more than 200 topics ranging from Asquith and Anarchism to Washington, George and Washington DC, no politician need ever go naked into the debating chamber, nor anyone enter a heated exchange unarmed by the best words of centuries past.

And let's not forget, it's also for the rest of us who like nothing more than a good old serendipitous browse.

If compiling dictionaries of quotations is my part-time

job, actually writing the jokes – or finding the quotes – is my day job. I work for personalities, performers and politicians to help them appear wittier – and/or wiser – than they may actually be in what passes for real life.

It's a job which can normally be done here at my desk but which has also taken me into the Houses of Parliament and No. 10, into Zsa Zsa Gabor's sprawling kitchenette in Beverly Hills and even halfway up the Amazon, helping Jamie Lee Curtis describe how she was feeling as she wrestled heroically with a semi-conscious anaconda. Pretending you're about to be crushed to death by a limbless reptile which is clearly struggling to keep its eyes open – now that's what I call acting!

Sometimes the call comes when you're doing something else with your life. I've written last-minute material in the Sydney Opera House; while motorcycling through Hungary; in a McDonalds on Hollywood Boulevard; and in a small-town library just off the A1(M).

It was in the local library that I wrote a tribute to the comedian Ronnie Barker, who'd died earlier that day. An old friend of his was appearing live on the ITN evening news and needed a few heartfelt words of tribute. An appropriate spoonerism – Ronnie loved his spoonerisms – was what I most hoped for. With the help of the librarian, I unearthed one at 5.30, with only minutes to spare. Standing on the steps of the library as Ronnie's friend dashed into make-up at ITN, I yelled into the phone, above the roar of the High Street traffic, 'Here it is:

Newsreader: So how do you think Ronnie's friends and family will take the news?

Friend: For them it will be a blushing crow.'

By contrast, some years ago I received an urgent, last-minute request from No. 10. George Bush Sr, President of the United States, was popping in later in the day for lunch and the Prime Minister needed a few Anglo-American quips and quotes for his welcome speech. No rush, but they'd call me back in half an hour. My mission: to amuse the most powerful man in the world in thirty minutes from ... NOW!

Now that's the sort of deadline that gets the brain cells fizzing with fear and trepidation, anxious beads of sweat splashing off my forehead onto the keyboard below.

If you're engaged in a debate, there should be enough quotes here to kindle the flame of contention and keep it afire.

I've aimed as far as possible for balance, including, where I can, a range of quotes reflecting both sides of any argument.

Be warned, though. A single well-turned quotation can sometimes – without warning – change your opinion. A view you'd always considered risible, if amusing, you might suddenly find convincing (with bad luck, right in the middle of the debate!).

So never underestimate the power of a counter-quote. A Lib Dem friend of mine stumbled upon an anti-quote while looking for a pro-quote and he's voted UKIP ever since – with devastating effects on the balance of power within his family.

So handle with care! Treat each of the quotations in this dictionary as a ticking time bomb. An otherwise innocent quotation can explode in your brain unexpectedly, changing your beliefs forever, at the moment you thought you were finally sure of them.

That's humour at work, ever ready to undermine your most precious and long-held beliefs. It thinks it's funny!

Many's the time I have seen an argument collapse like a deck of cards when a truer truth is suddenly revealed by a witty quotation. Things can get very messy, tears may flow and age-old certainties fold like a punctured concertina.

Where possible I have endeavoured with each quote to provide an exact contextual date and other details. Where this has not been possible, I have included the birth and death dates of the quotee alongside brief biographical details.

For misquotations, misidentified authors and other mistakes in the text, I take full responsibility. If you know better than me – or more than me – get in touch via Biteback.

I'll be happy to hear from you.

And you can quote me!

Fred Metcalf

A

#AGRICULTURE

Nobody is qualified to become a statesman who is entirely ignorant of the problem of wheat.
> Socrates, c.470–c.399 BC, Athenian philosopher

Grain is the currency of currencies.
> Vladimir Ilich Lenin, 1870–1924, Russian Marxist revolutionary and political theorist

The farmer will never be happy again;
He carries his heart in his boots;
For either the rain is destroying his grain
Or the drought is destroying his roots.
> A. P. Herbert, 1890–1971, 'The Farmer', 1922

Kansas had better stop raising corn and begin raising hell.
> Mary Elizabeth Lease, 1853–1933, American orator and agrarian reformer (attrib.)

No one hates his job so heartily as a farmer.
> H. L. Mencken, 1880–1956, American essayist and critic

A farm is an irregular patch of nettles bounded by short-term notes, containing a fool and his wife who didn't know enough to stay in the city.

S. J. Perelman, 1904–79, American humorist

No man should be allowed to be President who does not understand hogs, or has not been around a manure pile.

Harry S. Truman, 1884–1972, 33rd President of the United States, 1945–53

Farming looks mighty easy when your plough is a pencil, and you're a thousand miles from the corn field.

Dwight D. Eisenhower, 1890–1969, 34th President of the United States, 1953–61

He was a long-limbed farmer, a God-fearing, freedom-loving, law-abiding, rugged individualist who held that federal aid to anyone but farmers was creeping socialism.

Joseph Heller, 1923–99, *Catch 22*, 1961

#AID

Foreign Aid – taxing poor people in rich countries for the benefit of rich people in poor countries.

Bernard Rosenberg, 1923–96, Professor of Sociology, City College, New York, editor of *Dissent* magazine

Humanitarian aid in the US has begun arriving in Lebanon. The US Government sent 10,000 medical kits, 20,000 blankets, $30 million cash, and today the people of New Orleans said: 'They did *what*?'

Jay Leno, late-night talk-show host, 2006

It is easy to be conspicuously 'compassionate' if others are being forced to pay the cost.
> Murray Rothbard, 1926–95, American economist, historian and political theorist

No people do so much harm as those who go about doing good.
> Mandell Creighton, 1843–1901, British historian and Bishop of London

She's the sort of woman who lives for others. You can always tell the others by their hunted expression!
> C. S. Lewis, 1898–1963, British novelist, poet and theologian

High-toned humanitarians constantly overestimate the sufferings of those they sympathise with.
> H. L. Mencken, *Minority Report*, 1956

#AMERICA AND AMERICANS

I am willing to love all mankind – except an American.
> Samuel Johnson, 1709–84, English essayist, editor and lexicographer

I tremble for my country when I reflect that God is just.
> Thomas Jefferson, 1743–1826, 3rd President of the United States, 1801–09

In the United States there is more space where nobody is than where anybody is. That is what makes America what it is.
> Gertrude Stein, 1874–1946, American writer

America is a mistake, a giant mistake.

> Sigmund Freud, 1856–1939, Austrian physician and
> psychoanalyst

America is a large, friendly dog in a very small room. Every time it wags its tail, it knocks over a chair.

> Arnold J. Toynbee, 1889–1975, English historian

*Once there was one of those witty Frenchmen whose name
I cannot for the moment recall,
Who wittily remarked that America is the only country in
history that has passed directly from barbarism to decadence
without passing through civilization at all,
A remark which is wittily repeated with enthusiasm frantic
In the lands on the other side of the Atlantic,
And is, I suppose, more or less true,
Depending on the point of view.*

> Ogden Nash, 'Civilization is Constant Vexation', 1934

The American people, taking one with another, constitute the most timorous, snivelling, poltroonish, ignominious mob of serfs and goose-steppers ever gathered under one flag in Christendom since the end of the Middle Ages.

> H. L. Mencken, *Prejudices*, Third series, 1922

Being a great power is no longer much fun.

> David Schoenbaum, American social scientist and historian, *New York Times*, 1973

Losing is the great American sin.

> John Tunis, 1889–1975, sports fiction writer, quoted in the *New York Times*, 1977

I don't know much about Americanism, but it's a damn good word with which to carry an election.

Warren G. Harding, 1865–1923, 29th President of the United States, 1921–23

Of course, America had often been discovered before, but it had always been hushed up.

Oscar Wilde, 1854–1900, Irish playwright

... a nation that has given the world both nuclear weapons AND SpongeBob SquarePants.

Dave Barry, *Miami Herald*

The only thing that enables Belgium to be Belgium and Norway to be Norway and Britain to be Britain is the fact that America's America.

Mark Steyn, *Face of the Tiger*

... because it's the world's first non-imperial superpower the world has had to concoct a thesis that America is a threat not merely to this or that nation state but to the entire planet, and not because of conventional great-power designs but because – even scarier – of its 'consumption', its very way of life. Those Cokes and cheeseburgers detested by discriminating London novelists are devastating the planet in ways that straightforward genocidal conquerors like Hitler and Stalin could only have dreamed of. The construct of this fantasy is very revealing about how unthreatening America is.

Mark Steyn, *OC Register*

Americans are rather like bad Bulgarian wine: they don't travel well.

Bernard Falk, 1943–90, British author and television reporter

All America has to do to get in bad all over the world is just to start out on what we think is a Good Samaritan mission.
  Will Rogers, 1879–1935, American commentator and humorist

What a pity, when Christopher Columbus discovered America, that he ever mentioned it.
  Margot Asquith, 1864–1945, Anglo-Scottish socialite and wit

America is so vast that almost everything said about it is likely to be true, and the opposite is probably equally true.
  James T. Farrell, 1904–79, American novelist

Every time Europe looks across the Atlantic to see the American eagle, it observes only the rear end of an ostrich.
  H. G. Wells, 1866–1946, British science fiction writer

The United States is the greatest single achievement of European civilisation.
  Robert Balmain Mowat, 1883–1941, *The United States of America*, 1938

America is a vast conspiracy to make you happy.
  John Updike, 1932–2009, *Problems*, 1979

America wasn't founded so that we could all be better. America was founded so we could all be anything we damned well pleased.
  P. J. O'Rourke, libertarian journalist and commentator

I don't believe there's any problem in this country, no matter how tough it is, that Americans, when they roll up their sleeves, can't completely ignore.
  George Carlin, 1937–2008, *Brain Droppings*, 1997

I celebrated Thanksgiving in an old-fashioned way. I invited everyone in my neighbourhood to my house, we had an enormous feast, and then I killed them and took their land.
Jon Stewart, *The Daily Show*, Comedy Central

According to the latest poll, a record 73 per cent of Americans think the country is headed in the wrong direction. But the good news: gas is so expensive that we'll never get there.
Jay Leno

The American is the Englishman left to himself.
Alexis de Tocqueville, 1805–59, French political thinker and historian, 15 January 1832

#ANARCHISM

An anarchist is anyone who believes in less government than you do.
Robert LeFevre, 1911–86, American libertarian radio personality

#APPEASEMENT

An appeaser is one who feeds a crocodile hoping it will eat him last.
Winston Churchill, 1874–1965, British statesman, orator and writer

No people in history have ever survived who thought they could protect their freedom by making themselves inoffensive to their enemies.

>   Dean Acheson, 1893–1971, lawyer and United States
>   Secretary of State, 1949–53

No man can tame a tiger into a kitten by stroking it.

>   Franklin D. Roosevelt, 1882–1945, 32nd President of the
>   United States, 1933–45, *Fireside Chat*, 1940

The one sure way to conciliate a tiger is to allow oneself to be devoured.

>   Konrad Adenauer, 1876–1967, Chancellor of Germany,
>   1949–63

Appeasers believe that if you keep on throwing steaks to a tiger, the tiger will become a vegetarian.

>   Heywood Broun, 1888–1939, American newspaper
>   columnist and editor

#ARISTOCRACY

We adore titles and heredities in our hearts and ridicule them with our mouths. This is our democratic privilege.

>   Mark Twain, 1835–1910, American writer and humorist

Democracy means government by the uneducated, while aristocracy means government by the badly educated.

>   G. K. Chesterton, 1874–1936, *New York Times*, 1931

I've been offered titles but I think they get one into disreputable company.

>   George Bernard Shaw, 1856–1950, Irish playwright

#ARMY, THE

For it's Tommy this and Tommy that, an' 'Chuck him out, the brute!'
But it's 'Saviour of 'is country' when the guns begin to shoot.
    Rudyard Kipling, 'Tommy', 1892

Your friend the British soldier can stand up to anything except the British War Office.
    George Bernard Shaw, *The Devil's Disciple*, 1901

I didn't fire him because he was a dumb son of a bitch, although he was, but that's not against the law for generals. If it was, half to three-quarters of them would be in jail.
    Harry S. Truman

I have spent much of my life fighting the Germans and fighting the politicians. It is much easier to fight the Germans.
    Field Marshal Lord Montgomery, 1887–1976, *The Observer*, 1967

When I first went into the active Army you could tell someone to move a chair across the room – now you have to tell him why.
    Major Robert Lembke, 1913–89, quoted in *Newsweek*, 1979

I'm still recovering from a shock. I was nearly drafted. It's not that I mind fighting for my country, but they called me at a ridiculous time: in the middle of a war.
    Jackie Mason, American stand-up comedian

I had a very distinguished army career. I fought with Mountbatten in Burma. I fought with Alexander in Tunis. I fought with Montgomery at Alamein. I couldn't get on with anybody!

   Anon.

See also: DEFENCE, IRAQ WAR, MILITARY, NUCLEAR WAR, PEACE AND PACIFISM, WAR

#ASQUITH, HERBERT, 1852–1928, LIBERAL PRIME MINISTER, 1908–16

For twenty years Herbert Asquith has held a season ticket on the line of least resistance and has gone wherever the train of events has carried him, lucidly justifying his position at whatever point he has found himself.

   Leo Amery, 1873–1955, Conservative politician and
   journalist

#ATTLEE, CLEMENT, 1883–1967, LABOUR PRIME MINISTER, 1945–51

He is a modest little man with much to be modest about.

   Winston Churchill (attrib.)

What can you do with a man who looks like a female llama surprised while bathing?

   Winston Churchill

Charisma? He did not recognise the word except as a clue in his beloved *Times* crossword.
James Margach, *The Abuse of Power*, 1981

... reminds me of nothing so much as a dead fish before it has had time to stiffen.
George Orwell, 1903–50, British author and journalist (attrib.)

... a sheep in sheep's clothing.
Winston Churchill (attrib.)

An empty taxi arrived at 10 Downing Street, and when the door was opened, Attlee got out.
Anon.; often wrongly attributed to Winston Churchill

Few thought he was even a starter.
There were many who thought themselves smarter.
But he ended PM, CH and OM,
An Earl and a Knight of the Garter.
Clement Attlee (on his own political career)

He'd never use one syllable where none would do.
Douglas Jay, 1907–96, fellow British Labour Party politician

Clement Attlee brings to the fierce struggle of politics the tepid enthusiasm of a lazy summer afternoon at a cricket match.
Aneurin Bevan, 1897–1960, Welsh Labour politician and Cabinet minister under Attlee

See also: COMMUNISM, CUBA, DEMOCRAT SLOGANS, DEMOCRATIC PARTY, DEMOCRATS V. REPUBLICANS, DEMOCRATS, EQUALITY, LABOUR PARTY, LEFT V. RIGHT, LEFT, MARXISM, SOCIALISM V. CAPITALISM, SOCIALISM

#AUSTRALIA AND AUSTRALIANS

The average Australian politician wouldn't know a tram was up him unless the bell rang.
    Les Patterson, fictional Australian diplomat and bon viveur

In Australia, not reading poetry is the national pastime.
    Phyllis McGinley, 1905–78, American children's writer
    and poet

They say a well-balanced Australian is one with a chip on both shoulders.
    Anon.

I wonder if people in Australia call the rest of the world, 'Up over'.
    George Carlin, 1937–2008, American comedian

To live in Australia permanently is rather like going to a party and dancing all night with one's mother.
    Barry Humphries, Australian writer, performer and wit

Australia is an outdoor country. People only go inside to use the toilet. And that's only a recent development.
    Barry Humphries

The Australian language is easier to learn than boat talk. It has a vocabulary of about six words.

P. J. O'Rourke, *Holidays in Hell*, 1989

In America, only the successful writer is important; in France all writers are important; in England no writer is important; and in Australia you have to explain what a writer is.

Geoffrey Cotterell, 1919–2010, novelist

Heckler: I wouldn't vote for you if you were the Archangel Gabriel!
Menzies: If I were the Archangel Gabriel you wouldn't be in my constituency.

Robert Menzies, 1894–1978, Australian Liberal Party
Prime Minister

Never take any notice of anonymous letters, unless you get a few thousand on the same subject.

Robert Menzies

Out in the bush, the tarred road always ends just after the house of the local mayor.

Anon.

There is nothing more Australian than spending time in somebody else's country.

Anon.

A fair go for all, regardless of ethnicity, race, religion, except for Poms, Seppos and Kiwis.

Australian slogan; anon.

... like being flogged with a warm lettuce.
> Paul Keating, Labor Prime Minister, of Liberal–National
> coalition leader John Hewson

Always back the horse named self-interest, son. It'll be the
only one trying.
> Jack Lang, 1876–1975, Labor Premier of New South Wales

It may be that your sole purpose in life is to serve as a
warning to others.
> Anonymous Australian

... like a lizard on a rock, alive but looking dead.
> Paul Keating, of Liberal–National coalition leader John
> Hewson

You look like an Easter Island statue with an arse full of
razor blades.
> Paul Keating, of Liberal Prime Minister Malcolm Fraser

#AXIOMS AND ADVICE

No man ever became great or good except through many
and great mistakes.
> William Ewart Gladstone, 1809–98, four-time Liberal
> Prime Minister

The art of politics consists in knowing precisely when it is
necessary to hit an opponent slightly below the belt.
> Konrad Adenauer

People who think they know everything are a great annoyance to those of us who do.

Isaac Asimov, 1919–82, American author and scientist

It is never wise to try to appear to be more clever than you are. It is sometimes wise to appear slightly less so.

William Whitelaw, 1918–99, Conservative Cabinet minister

A thick skin is a gift from God.

Konrad Adenauer

Talk to a man about himself and he will listen for hours.

Benjamin Disraeli, 1804–81, writer and Conservative
Prime Minister, 1874–80

I dream of a better tomorrow, where chickens can cross the road and not be questioned about their motives.

Anon.

If you don't say anything, you won't be called upon to repeat it.

Calvin Coolidge, 1872–1933, 30th President of the United
States, 1923–29

There's no end to what you can accomplish if you don't care who gets the credit.

Anon.

Don't go around saying the world owes you a living. The world owes you nothing. It was here first.

Mark Twain

The greatest lesson in life is to know that even fools are right sometimes.
    Winston Churchill

Keep the dream alive: Hit the snooze button.
    Anon.

Being wrong is one of the privileges of public life and indeed it is widely practised.
    Tony Benn, Labour Cabinet minister

It is only when one begins to write things down that one sees the wisdom of not writing them down.
    Norman Lamont, Conservative MP and Chancellor of the Exchequer

Bringing the leadership to its knees occasionally is a good way of keeping it on its toes.
    Tony Banks, 1942–2006, Labour MP and Cabinet minister

Friends may come and friends may go, but enemies accumulate.
    Anon.

There are three things in this world you can do nothing about: getting Aids, getting clamped and running out of Chateau Lafite '45.
    Alan Clark, 1928–99, Conservative MP and diarist

Never murder a man when he's busy committing suicide.
    Woodrow Wyatt, 1918–97, Labour MP and columnist

There is nothing more dangerous than to leap a chasm in two jumps.

David Lloyd George, 1863–1945, Liberal Prime Minister, 1916–22 (attrib.)

It is a good thing to follow the First Law of Holes: if you are in one, stop digging.

Denis Healey, Labour Chancellor of the Exchequer, 1974–79, in 1983

B

#BALDWIN, STANLEY, 1867–1947, CONSERVATIVE PRIME MINISTER, 1923-24, 1924-29, 1935-37

Decided only to be undecided, resolved to be irreso-
lute, adamant for drift, solid for fluidity, all-powerful to
be impotent.
  Winston Churchill, 1874–1965, British statesman, orator
  and writer

A man of the utmost insignificance.
  Lord Curzon, 1859–1925, Conservative statesman

He occasionally stumbled over the truth, but hastily picked
himself up and hurried on as if nothing had happened.
  Winston Churchill

I think Baldwin has gone mad. He simply takes one jump in
the dark; looks round; and then takes another.
  F. E. Smith, 1st Earl of Birkenhead, 1872–1930, lawyer,
  orator, Conservative statesman, letter to Austen
  Chamberlain, 1923

One could not even dignify him with the name of stuffed shirt. He was simply a hole in the air.

George Orwell, 'The Lion and the Unicorn: Socialism and the English Genius', 1941

This second-rate orator trails his tawdry wisps of mist over the parliamentary scene.

Aneurin Bevan, 1897–1960, Labour Cabinet minister

#BALLS, ED, AND YVETTE COOPER, SHADOW CHANCELLOR OF THE EXCHEQUER AND SHADOW HOME SECRETARY

... Balls is said to be fantastically clever, a master of strategy, a seer for the Centre Left. Despite these horizon-scanning gifts, he looks permanently surprised, less the learned prophet than a man whose breakfast has just gone down the wrong way after receiving a nasty surprise from the electricity bill.

Quentin Letts, *50 People Who Buggered Up Britain*, 2008

... Balls is good at ignoring things. He is covered in a transparent varnish which sometimes makes him impervious to other points of view and to mocking laughter.

Quentin Letts, *50 People Who Buggered Up Britain*, 2008

... The Ballses are high Brahmins of the modern elite and it is their presumption, their lack of understanding for the 'lower orders' of the country they casually think they will govern, which makes them such an insufferable and dangerous menace.

Quentin Letts, *50 People Who Buggered Up Britain*, 2008

Nowhere will you see two women address each other with such wintry disdain as Theresa May and Yvette Cooper do in the Commons. The moment they start exchanging their scornful barbs, the temperature drops forty degrees. Icicles glitter from the ceiling. Freezing gusts whistle between the benches. The Speaker's interventions are drowned out by the chatter of MPs' teeth. Up in the press gallery, hacks huddle for warmth round a bonfire of order papers. It's like Narnia, but with two White Witches.

... Mrs May rose. The temperature plummeted another ten degrees. A backbencher keeled over with frostbite and had to be dragged out of the chamber on a sled. The Serjeant-at-Arms stumbled in the snow and was devoured by a passing polar bear.

Michael Deacon, *Daily Telegraph*, 2012

See also: GORDON BROWN, LABOUR PARTY, SOCIALISM

#BANKS AND BANKING

An investment banker said he was going to concentrate on the big issues from now on. He sold me one in the street yesterday.

Anon.

Bankers are people that help you with problems you would not have had without them.

Anon.

Banking may well be a career from which no man really recovers.

John Kenneth Galbraith, 1908–2006, Canadian-American economist

... they all observe one rule which woe betides the banker
who fails to heed it,
Which is you must never lend any money to anybody unless
they don't need it.
    Ogden Nash, 1902–71, 'Bankers are Just Like Anybody
    Else, except Richer', 1938

There is no group of people on the planet more stupid
than bankers. They should be called bonkers. Look at the
famous banks that are suddenly losing billions, because
they handed out loans like lunatics.
    Michael Winner, English film director, 2008

See also: BIG BUSINESS, BUSINESS, CAPITALISM,
CREDIT CRUNCH, ECONOMICS AND ECONOMISTS,
ECONOMY, GORDON BROWN, INFLATION, LABOUR
PARTY, MONEY, OCCUPY MOVEMENT, POVERTY,
RICH AND POOR, STOCK MARKET AND WALL
STREET, TAXATION, WEALTH

#BENN, TONY, LABOUR MINISTER OF TECHNOLOGY, 1966–70

I have always said this of Tony: he immatures with age.
    Harold Wilson, 1916–95, Labour Prime Minister, 1964–70,
    1974–76, in 1981

It's the same each time with progress. First they ignore you,
then they say you're mad, then dangerous, then there's
a pause and then you can't find anyone who disagrees
with you.
    Tony Benn

I am on the right wing of the middle of the road and with a strong radical bias.
   Tony Benn

#BEVAN, ANEURIN, 1897–1960, LABOUR MINISTER OF HEALTH, 1945–51

Unless the right honourable gentleman changes his policy and methods and moves without the slightest delay, he will be as great a curse to this country in peace as he was a squalid nuisance in time of war.
   Winston Churchill, while Leader of the Conservative
   Opposition, 1945

This island is made mainly of coal and surrounded by fish. Only an organising genius could produce a shortage of coal and fish at the same time.
   Aneurin Bevan, speech, May 1945

He enjoys prophesying the end of the capitalist system and is prepared to play a part, any part, in its burial except that of a mute.
   Harold Macmillan, 1894–1986, Conservative Prime
   Minister, 1957–63 (attrib.)

Not while I'm alive, he ain't.
   Ernest Bevin, 1881–1951, British trades union leader and
   Labour politician, on hearing it said that fellow minister
   Aneurin Bevan was 'his own worst enemy' (attrib.)

See also: COMMUNISM, EQUALITY, LABOUR PARTY, LEFT V. RIGHT, LEFT, LIBERAL PARTY, LIBERALS

AND LIBERALISM, LIBERALS V. CONSERVATIVES, MARXISM, SOCIALISM V CAPITALISM, SOCIALISM

#BIDEN, JOE, VICE PRESIDENT UNDER BARACK OBAMA

Joe Biden is Barack Obama's running mate. Yeah, nothing says change like a guy who's been in the Senate for thirty-five years.

David Letterman, late-night talk-show host, 2008

Obama said that he says a brief prayer every morning, but then Joe Biden shows up anyway. So I don't know if it would really work.

Jay Leno, late-night talk-show host, 2011

President Obama was in Disney World today where he unveiled his new plan to create jobs. He was joined by Mickey Mouse and Minnie Mouse but not Goofy. He had to stay behind to tend to his Vice-Presidential duties.

Jay Leno, 2011

Iran is now in possession of an American drone. When I heard that I thought, 'Oh, my God, they captured Joe Biden!'

Jay Leno, 2011

Happy Birthday to Vice President Biden, who turns sixty-nine this weekend! When they saw him coming, White House staffers turned off the lights, hid behind the couch. And then waited for him to leave.

Jimmy Fallon, late-night talk-show host, 2011

Conrad Murray was found guilty of giving Michael Jackson
an overdose of a prescription sleeping aid. Pretty reckless on
the part of the doctor. They said the sedative he prescribed
was five times more powerful than a Joe Biden speech.
 Jay Leno, 2012

See also: BARACK OBAMA, VICE PRESIDENCY

#BIG BUSINESS

We could manage to survive without money changers
and stockbrokers. We should find it harder to do without
miners, steel workers and those who cultivate the land.
 Aneurin Bevan, *In Place of Fear*, 1952

In government, Mr McCain has always been a good friend
of the big corporations.
 I'd be amazed if they haven't named a tax loophole
after him.
 Anon., of John McCain, Republican Presidential nominee,
 2008

Corporation: an ingenious device for obtaining individual
profit without individual responsibility.
 Ambrose Bierce, *The Devil's Dictionary*, 1911

See also: BANKS AND BANKING, BUSINESS,
CAPITALISM, CREDIT CRUNCH, ECONOMICS
AND ECONOMISTS, ECONOMY, INFLATION,
MONEY, POVERTY, RICH AND POOR, STOCK
MARKET AND WALL STREET, TAXATION, WEALTH

#BIN LADEN, OSAMA

Obama killed bin Laden like Nixon landed on the moon.
  John Bolton, Republican lawyer and diplomat, 2012

More bad news for the Taliban. Remember how they are
promised seventy-two virgins when they die? Turns out that
it's only one 72-year-old virgin.
  Jay Leno, 2011

Osama bin Laden has ten lookalikes to fool us Americans.
Ten lookalikes – and he's married to five of them.
  David Letterman, 2011

The FBI announced today that they are now looking for
Osama bin Laden's financial advisor. You think this guy is
in demand. How good can he be? His top client is living in a
cave and driving a donkey. It doesn't sound like he is getting
the best return on his investments to me.
  Jay Leno

After all the talk about caves, bin Laden was hiding in a
million-dollar mansion in Pakistan. The CIA became suspicious when they learned there was a million-dollar mansion
in Pakistan.
  Jimmy Kimmel, late-night talk-show host, 2011

There's already been some trouble for Osama bin Laden
in the afterlife. There was a mix-up and he was greeted by
seventy-two vegans.
  David Letterman, 2011

The SEALs recovered an extensive stash of pornography from bin Laden's compound. It's probably not easy just having sex with the same eleven wives all the time. There were interesting titles: *Debby Does Abbottabad, Deep Goat, Bare Ankles 4*, and *2 Humps, 1 Camel*.

Jimmy Fallon, *Late Night with Jimmy Fallon*, NBC, May 2011

See also: IRAQ WAR, WAR ON TERROR

#BIRTH CONTROL

GUNS DON'T KILL PEOPLE.
ABORTION CLINICS KILL PEOPLE.
Bumper sticker, Florida, 2006

ABORTION.
IT'S NOT A CHOICE, IT'S AN INDUSTRY.
Bumper sticker, New Orleans, 2005

KEEP YOUR ROSARIES OUT OF OUR OVARIES.
Slogan, Women's Action Committee against anti-abortionists, 1992

#BLAIR, TONY, LABOUR PRIME MINISTER, 1997–2007

I believe Tony Blair is an out-and-out rascal, terminally untrustworthy and close to being unhinged... To the extent that he even believes what he says, he is delusional. To the extent that he does not, he is an actor whose first invention – himself – has been his only interesting role.

Matthew Parris, former Conservative MP, *The Times*, 2006

I view him as the kind of air-guitarist of political rhetoric.
  Will Self, novelist, BBC Radio, 2006

You want to believe in Tony Blair, but rather like if you want to believe in God, there are times when he makes it very difficult to believe.
  Rory Bremner, British comedian and impressionist

It is just flipping unbelievable. He is a mixture of Harry Houdini and a greased piglet. He is barely human in his elusiveness. Nailing Blair is like trying to pin jelly to a wall.
  Boris Johnson, Conservative Mayor of London, *Daily Telegraph*, 2004

He's lost the plot, people tell me. He's drifting rudderless in the wide Sargasso Sea of New Labour's ideological vacuum ... Blair dead in the water? No such luck.
  Boris Johnson, *Daily Telegraph*, 2004

Tony Blair has a smile like an ageing collie.
  Jan Morris, British travel writer

Tony Blair is so weak and vulnerable now, Madonna is thinking of adopting him.
  Rory Bremner

Tony Blair does the work of two men – Laurel and Hardy.
  Bob Monkhouse, 1928–2003, English comedian

I have some exciting news. In Britain, in a democratic election, Tony Blair has been rewarded with a third term as
Prime Minister. And I just want to say for me – I'm sorry.
It's a little emotional to see democracy flourish in that part
of the world. I'm not saying that it's because of the Iraq War
– but it happened after. They said that you couldn't bring
democracy to those scone-eating, tea-drinking bastards and
I said, 'No, everyone yearns to be free.'
> Jon Stewart, American comic and commentator, 2005

He was the future, once.
> David Cameron, Conservative leader, at their first exchange
> in the House of Commons, 2005

It was announced in England that Tony Blair will leave
as British Prime Minister in May. So, President Bush has
toppled yet another government.
> Jay Leno, 2006

It's been reported that British Prime Minister Tony Blair
is going to be stepping down next summer. After hearing
about it, President Bush said, 'Damn, he's the only foreign
guy who speaks American.'
> Conan O'Brien, late-night talk-show host, 2006

Tony Blair, Prime Minister of England, is stepping down.
He said he wanted to spend more time humping Bush's
leg. He said he hopes people remember him as the people's
poodle ... They didn't have the heart to tell Bush. They
didn't say Blair was gone. They just said he went to live on
a farm.
> Bill Maher, late-night talk-show host, 2006

Future generations will use Blair's name as a swearword so offensive it currently has no equivalent in the English language.
Charlie Brooker, journalist, *The Guardian*, 2007

Tony Blair has done more U-turns than a dodgy plumber.
Iain Duncan Smith, former Conservative leader, on Tony Blair's attitude to Europe, 2003

He may be a liar but he's the people's liar.
Andy Hamilton, English comedian and writer

With Tony you have to take the smooth with the smooth.
Anonymous Labour politician

I keep a video of Tony Blair reading Corinthians at Diana's funeral and threaten to show it to anyone who is impressed by the PM's sincerity.
Bob Marshall-Andrews, lawyer and backbench Labour MP

There is a good, rough word to describe Tony Blair but we had better not write it out here in full. Let us just say that he's a selfish w***** and that he'll be forgotten about long before Westminster vanishes from the political map.
Quentin Letts, *50 People Who Buggered Up Britain*, 2008

See also: GORDON BROWN, COMMUNISM, EQUALITY, IRAQ WAR, LABOUR PARTY, LEFT V. RIGHT, LEFT, LIBERAL PARTY, LIBERALS AND LIBERALISM, LIBERALS V. CONSERVATIVES, MARXISM, SOCIALISM V. CAPITALISM, SOCIALISM

#BRITAIN AND THE BRITISH

When I warned them (the French Government) that Britain would fight on alone whatever they did, their Generals told their PM and his divided Cabinet: 'In three weeks England will have her neck wrung like a chicken.' Some chicken! Some neck!

   Winston Churchill, speech, Canadian Parliament, 1941

To disagree with three fourths of the British public on all points is one of the first elements of sanity, one of the deepest consolations in all moments of spiritual doubt.

   Oscar Wilde, 1854–1900, Irish playwright

... a soggy little island, huffing and puffing to keep up with Western Europe.

   John Updike, 1932–2009, American novelist

One of my ministers found half-naked with a guardsman in Hyde Park? Last Wednesday? The coldest night of the year? Makes you proud to be British!

   Winston Churchill

In peacetime the British may have many faults; but so far an inferiority complex has not been one of them.

   Lord Gladwyn, 1900–96, British diplomat and civil servant, *The Observer*, 1967

The British public has always had an unerring taste for ungifted amateurs.

   John Osborne, 1929–94, English playwright, 1957

See also: ENGLAND AND THE ENGLISH, IRELAND
AND THE IRISH, SCOTLAND AND THE SCOTS,
WALES AND THE WELSH

#BROWN, GORDON, LABOUR PRIME MINISTER, 2007–10

Allowing Gordon Brown into No. 10 would be like letting
Mrs Rochester out of the attic. He has no empathy with
people and you need that to be Prime Minister.
  Frank Field, Labour MP, 2007

You're an analogue politician in a digital age.
  David Cameron, 2006

The Conservatives have clearly now realised that looks are
important: the party's latest posters depict Gordon Brown,
his face decked out, as ever these days, with the kind of
grin that looks as if it had to be fastened into position
using discreet safety pins. Mr Brown is yet to note the link
between his chilling pseudo-smile and his public approval
rating. Ten years ago, when he never smiled, the public
broadly trusted him; now that he always smiles, it doesn't.
His best hope of retaining power is to go back to looking
as he did in the 1990s, i.e. like a bad-tempered wardrobe
in a suit.
  Michael Deacon, *Daily Telegraph*, March 2010

The House has noticed the Prime Minister's remarkable transformation in the last few weeks from Stalin to Mr Bean, creating chaos out of order instead of order out of chaos.
> Vince Cable, Liberal Democrat politician, of Gordon
> Brown, speech in the House of Commons, 2007

Like all politicians, I don't bear grudges. I learned that from Gordon.
> Ed Miliband, leader of the Labour Party, at Lobby
> lunch, 2012

See also: TONY BLAIR, COMMUNISM, EQUALITY, LABOUR PARTY, LEFT V. RIGHT, LEFT, LIBERAL PARTY, LIBERALS AND LIBERALISM, LIBERALS V. CONSERVATIVES, MARXISM, SOCIALISM V. CAPITALISM, SOCIALISM

#BUREAUCRACY

I do not rule Russia. Ten thousand clerks do.
> Nicholas I, 1796–1855, Emperor of Russia 1825–55

It is an inevitable defect, that bureaucrats will care more for routine than for results.
> Walter Bagehot, 1826–77, *The English Constitution*, 1867

Bureaucracy is a giant mechanism operated by pygmies.
> Honoré de Balzac, 1799–1850, French novelist and
> playwright

The work of internal government has become the task of controlling the thousands of fifth-rate men.

Henry Adams, 1838–1918, American journalist, novelist and historian

Let's find out what everyone is doing,
And then stop everyone from doing it.

A. P. Herbert, 'Let's Stop Everyone from Doing Something!', 1930

Committee – a group of men who individually can do nothing but as a group decide that nothing can be done.

Fred Allen, 1894–1956, American comedian

Britain has invented a new missile. It's called the civil servant – it doesn't work and it can't be fired.

Anon.

Bureaucrats write memos both to look busy while writing and because the memos, once written, become proof that they were busy.

Daniel Hannan, Conservative MEP, 2012

Prominent Democrats seem to have great difficulty getting even the well-known bits (of religion) right. Christmas, according to Hillary Rodham Clinton in 1999, is when those in that particular faith tradition celebrate 'the birth of a homeless child'. Or, as Al Gore put it in 1997, 'Two thousand years ago, a homeless woman gave birth to a homeless child.' For Pete's sake, they weren't homeless – they couldn't get a hotel room. They had to sleep in the stable only because Dad had to schlep halfway across the country to pay his taxes in the town of his birth, which sounds like the kind of cockamamie bureaucratic nightmare only a blue state could cook up. Except that in Massachusetts, it's no doubt illegal to rent out your stable without applying for a Livestock Shelter Change of Use Permit plus a Temporary Maternity Ward for Non-Insured Transients License, so Mary would have been giving birth under a bridge on I-95.

Mark Steyn, *National Review*, 2004

We can lick gravity, but sometimes the paperwork is overwhelming.

Wernher von Braun, 1912–77, rocket scientist, *Chicago Sun-Times*, 1958

Bureaucracy is the epoxy that greases the wheels of government.

James H. Boren, 1925–2010, humorist and academic

Guidelines for bureaucrats: 1. When in charge, ponder. 2.When in trouble, delegate. 3 When in doubt, mumble.

James H. Boren, *New York Times*, 1970

The only thing that saves us from the bureaucracy is its inefficiency.

Eugene McCarthy, 1916–2005, American poet and politician

No Exit: a sign indicating the most convenient way out of a building.

Beachcomber, *Beachcomber: The Works of J. B. Morton*, 1974

In a hierarchy every employee tends to rise to his level of incompetence.

Laurence J. Peter, 1919–90, *The Peter Principle*, 1969

I think it will be a clash between the political will and the administrative won't.

Antony Jay and Jonathan Lynn, *Yes Minister*, 1987

You will never understand bureaucracies until you understand that for bureaucrats procedure is everything and outcomes are nothing.

Thomas Sowell, American economist and political
philosopher

... There's no problem in the world that can't be made worse by a corrupt, meddling, wasteful, politically correct bureaucracy trying to make things better.

James Delingpole, *Watermelons: How Environmentalists
are Killing the Planet, Destroying the Economy and
Stealing Your Children's Future*, 2011

See also: CIVIL SERVICE AND WHITEHALL,
GOVERNMENT, LOCAL GOVERNMENT

#BUSH, GEORGE H. W., 41ST PRESIDENT OF THE UNITED STATES, 1989-93

... the sort of man who steps out of the shower to take a piss.

Anonymous Texan

I do not like broccoli and I haven't liked it since I was a little kid and my mother made me eat it. And I'm President of the United States and I'm not going to eat any more broccoli.

Now look, this is the last statement I'm going to have on broccoli. There are truckloads of broccoli at this very minute descending on Washington. My family is divided. For the broccoli vote out there: Barbara loves broccoli. She

has tried to make me eat it. She eats it all the time herself. So she can go out and meet the caravan of broccoli that's coming in.
   George H. W. Bush, news conference, 1990

Poor George, he can't help it. He was born with a silver foot in his mouth.
   Ann Richards, 1933–2006, Democratic Governor of Texas,
   1991–95, in 1988

Anyone who eats pork rinds can't be all good.
   Barbara Bush, on husband George

I will never apologise for the United States – I don't care what the facts are ... I'm not an apologise-for-America kind of guy.
   George H. W. Bush, said as Vice President, 1988

I have opinions of my own, strong opinions. But I don't always agree with them.
   George H. W. Bush, also attributed to George W. Bush

See also: PRESIDENCY, WHITE HOUSE

#BUSH, GEORGE W., 43RD PRESIDENT OF THE UNITED STATES, 2001–09

President Bush has been working on his inauguration.
Not the actual speech but the word 'inaugural'.
   David Letterman, 2005

President Bush delivered his first State of the Union address, riding high on an 82 per cent approval rating, and with Attorney General John Ashcroft despatching agents to interview the other 18 per cent.

Jon Stewart, *The Daily Show*, 2001

Some sad news, President Bush's lapdog passed away. Gee, I didn't even know Tony Blair was sick!

Jay Leno, *The Tonight Show*, 2005

President Bush is not fazed by other candidates' war records. He said, I may have not fought in Vietnam, but I created one.

Craig Kilborn, *The Late, Late Show*, 2004

Every sentence he manages to utter scatters its component parts like pond water from a verb chasing its own tail.

Clive James, Australian poet and critic

Delivering the State of the Union? That bloke couldn't deliver pizza.

Clive James

George W. Bush has a new campaign slogan: 'A reformer with results.' I don't know what it means [but] I think it's better than his old campaign slogan: 'A dumb guy with connections.'

David Letterman, *The Late Show*, 2000

President Bush helped dedicate an aircraft carrier named after his father. Isn't that nice? He christened the ship by saying, 'It's great to be here on the USS Dad'.

Conan O'Brien, 2006

He's unusually incurious, abnormally unintelligent, amazingly inarticulate, fantastically uncultured, extraordinarily uneducated and apparently quite proud of all of these things.
   Christopher Hitchens, 1949–2011, *Hardball with Chris Matthews*, 2000

George Bush reminds every woman of her first husband.
   Jane O'Reilly, American feminist and humorist, 1984

According to reports, Fidel Castro is alert and being briefed. And I'm thinking, why didn't we get a President like that?
   David Letterman, 2006

George Bush doesn't know the names of countries, he doesn't know the names of foreign leaders and he can't even find the Earth on a globe.
   Doug Ferrari, American stand-up comedian

We need a President who's fluent in at least one language.
   Buck Henry, American actor, writer and film director

Calling George W. Bush shallow is like calling a dwarf short.
   Molly Ivins, 1944–2007, newspaper columnist and commentator

President Bush says he needs a month off to unwind. Unwind? When the hell does this guy *wind*?
   David Letterman

I want to start by saying something nice about President Bush. Of all the Presidents we've had with the last name of Bush, his economic plan ranks in the top two.

John Kerry, Democratic Party nominee in 2004 Presidential
Election with George W. Bush as his opponent

This is an impressive crowd: the haves, and the have-mores. Some people call you the elite, I call you my base.

George W. Bush, speech, Washington, 2000

President Bush is going to establish elections there in Iraq. He's going to rebuild the infrastructure. He's going to create jobs. He said if it works there, he'll try it here.

David Letterman, *The Late Show*, 2004

President Bush said that the people who are attacking our forces in Iraq are getting more and more desperate because we're making so much progress. So just remember, the worse it gets, the better it is.

Jay Leno, *The Tonight Show*, 2005

President Bush is asking Congress for 80 billion dollars to rebuild Iraq. And when you make out that cheque, remember there are two L's in Halliburton.

David Letterman, *The Late Show*, 2005

Bush is in command. When he heard that sectarian militias had killed Iraqis, he called for an immediate invasion of Sectaria.

Bill Maher, 2006

These stories about my intellectual capacity really get under my skin. You know, for a while I even thought my staff believed it. There on my schedule first thing every morning it said, 'Intelligence Briefing'.

George W. Bush, speech, Washington, 2001

Next time I tell you someone from Texas should not be President of the United States, please pay attention.

Molly Ivins

Bushisms

I know how hard it is for you to put food on your family.

George W. Bush, Greater Nashua, NH, Chamber of
Commerce, 27 January 2000

I've abandoned free market principles to save the free market system.

George W. Bush, Washington, DC, 16 December 2008

Rarely is the question asked: is our children learning?

George W. Bush, Florence, SC, 11 January 2000

Goodbye from the world's biggest polluter!

George W. Bush, parting words to British Prime Minister
Gordon Brown and French President Nicolas Sarkozy at
his final G8 Summit, Rusutsu, Japan, 10 July 2008

Let me start off by saying that in 2000 I said, 'Vote for me. I'm an agent of change.' In 2004, I said, 'I'm not interested in change – I want to continue as President.' Every candidate has got to say 'change'. That's what the American people expect.

George W. Bush, Washington, DC, 5 March 2008

They misunderestimated me.
George W. Bush, Bentonville, AR, 6 November 2000

Never again in the halls of Washington, DC, do I want to have to make explanations that I can't explain.
George W. Bush, Portland, OR, 31 October 2000

Families is where our nation finds hope, where wings take dream.
George W. Bush, LaCrosse, WI, 18 October 2000

It's clearly a budget. It's got a lot of numbers in it.
George W. Bush, *Reuters*, 5 May 2000

I know that the human being and the fish can coexist peacefully.
George W. Bush, Saginaw, MI, 29 September 2000

See also: PRESIDENCY, WHITE HOUSE

#BUSINESS

The business of government is to keep the government out of business – that is, unless business needs government aid.
Will Rogers, 1879–1935, American commentator and humorist

If the government was as afraid of disturbing the consumer as it is of disturbing business, this would be some democracy.
Kin Hubbard, 1868–1930, American cartoonist, humorist and journalist

Nothing is illegal if one hundred well-placed businessmen decide to do it.

    Andrew Young, Congressman and Mayor of Atlanta

Humans must breathe but corporations must make money.

    Alice Embree, Texan activist and organiser

Banking establishments are more dangerous than standing armies.

    Thomas Jefferson, 1743–1826, 3rd President of the United States, 1801–09

The craft of the merchant is to bring a thing from where it abounds to where it is costly.

    Ralph Waldo Emerson, 1803–82, American essayist, lecturer and poet

He [the businessman] is the only man who is forever apologising for his occupation.

    H. L. Mencken, 1880–1956, American essayist and critic

I never knew a politician to go wrong until he's been contaminated by contact with a businessman.

    Finley Peter Dunne, 1867–1936, American humorous writer

See also: BANKS AND BANKING, BIG BUSINESS, CAPITALISM, CREDIT CRUNCH, ECONOMICS AND ECONOMISTS, ECONOMY, INFLATION, MONEY, POVERTY, RICH AND POOR, STOCK MARKET AND WALL STREET, TAXATION, WEALTH

C

#CAMERON, DAVID, CONSERVATIVE PRIME MINISTER, 2010–

I have the most corny CV possible. It goes: Eton, Oxford,
Conservative Research Department, Treasury, Home Office,
Carlton TV and then Conservative MP.
  David Cameron, speaking in 2003

Cameron's actually a serious threat to me. He does Tony
Blair much better than I do.
  Rory Bremner, British comedian and impressionist, 2006

… confident, entitled, gracious, secure … exactly the kind of
'natural Etonian' I was not.
  James Wood, literary critic and Harvard professor

It seems to me he has lost the art of communication; but
not, alas, the gift of speech.
  Gordon Brown, Labour Prime Minister, 2007–10

… maddeningly sane … eloquently uncommunicative … he
trails a comet-tail of blandness as pungent as garlic.
  Matthew Parris, former Conservative MP, *The Times*,
  March 2011

He seems content-free to me. Never had a job, except in PR, and it shows. People ask, 'What do you think of him?' and my answer is: 'He doesn't make me think.'

Christopher Hitchens, British journalist and controversialist, on David Cameron, interviewed in the *New Statesman*, 2010

Nor can a news report remark on the peculiar hand gestures politicians make when at the Despatch Box ... David Cameron alternates between karate-chopping an imaginary loaf of bread, and caressing the waist of a slightly over-weight dance partner.

Michael Deacon, *Daily Telegraph*, 2011

On the subject of Europe more generally, he declared several times that 'change is coming', although enigmatically he never made quite clear what that change might entail; it was a bit like listening to an Old Etonian Bob Dylan.

Michael Deacon, *Daily Telegraph*, 2012 on David Cameron in the House of Commons

What is it about David Cameron that makes him so ... Dad-like? Obviously he has children, but I'm not talking about his family life. I'm talking about his public life. In the way he talks, acts and looks, there's something indefinably ... Daddish.

When he takes off his jacket and rolls up his sleeves, you find yourself thinking, 'Ooh, Daddy means business.' When he declares that he's going to protect Britain from the Eurozone crisis, you think, 'Don't worry, Daddy's here.' When his face reddens at the despatch box, you think, 'Uh-oh, Daddy's getting cross.' And when he's photo-graphed throwing his arms in the air to celebrate Chelsea winning the football, you think, 'Oh Daaaaad, pur-LEASE don't embarrass us...'

Michael Deacon, *Daily Telegraph*, 2012

Under pressure, he falls back on what any teacher could tell you is bad exam technique: instead of answering the question, he simply fires off anything he can think of on the given topic, whether relevant or not. Thus what he said was confident, fluent, and almost wholly specious.

Michael Deacon, *Daily Telegraph*, 2012, on Cameron at PMQs

I can't be the only one here who finds himself constantly driven to a state of planet-struck incomprehension by the sheer asininity, the counter-productivity, the gormlessness, the stupidity, the truly epic wrongness of almost every new policy the government introduces.

James Delingpole, *Daily Telegraph*, July 2012

... Cameron's Coalition is so obviously toast you could spread it with butter and eat it with kippers.

James Delingpole, *Daily Telegraph*, July 2012

See also: CONSERVATIVE PARTY, CONSERVATIVES, LIBERALS V. CONSERVATIVES, LIBERTARIANISM, LEFT V. RIGHT

#CAMPAIGNING

The senator got so tired on the campaign trail that he started kissing hands and shaking babies.

David Letterman, late-night talk-show host, not original

My opponent called me a cream puff ... Well, I rushed out and got the baker's union to endorse me.

Claiborne Pell, 1918–2009, Democratic Senator from Rhode Island, 1987

You campaign in poetry; you govern in prose.
>   Mario Cuomo, Democratic Governor of New York
>   1983–94, in 1985

We don't have to do what the candidates do: talk about huge issues in thirty seconds in a field somewhere, trying to make sure cows don't urinate on our shoes.
>   Mario Cuomo, talking about the Presidential campaign in
>   1988

A candidate could easily commit political suicide if he were to come up with an unconventional thought during a Presidential tour.
>   E. B. White, 1899–1985, American writer

Just think what my margin might have been if I had never left home at all.
>   John F. Kennedy, 1917–63, 35th President of the United
>   States, 1961–63, remarking on the fact that he had
>   campaigned hard in Alaska and lost, but won Hawaii
>   easily without visiting it

If you let Barnum and Bailey interpret a plot by Stendhal, it might come out to be something like the 1972 Democratic Convention.
>   Gloria Steinem, American journalist, feminist and activist,
>   'Campaigning', 1983

We were told our campaign wasn't sufficiently slick. We regard that as a compliment.
>   Margaret Thatcher, Conservative Prime Minister 1979–90

Campaign promises are – by long democratic tradition – the least binding form of human commitment.
  Antonin Scalia, United States Supreme Court judge, 2002

Have you ever seen a candidate talking to a rich person on television?
  Art Buchwald, 1925–2007, American humorous
  commentator

The only reason I'm not running for President is that I'm afraid no woman will come forward and say she's slept with me.
  Garry Shandling, American actor and comedian

See also: CANDIDATES, DEMOCRACY, ELECTIONS, MAJORITY, VOTING

#CANADA AND CANADIANS

Canada has never been a melting pot, more like a tossed salad.
  Arnold Edinborough, Canadian writer and lay preacher

In Pierre Elliott Trudeau, Canada has at last produced a political leader worthy of assassination.
  Irving Layton, 1912–2006, *The Whole Bloody Bird*, 1969

Americans are benevolently ignorant about Canada, while Canadians are malevolently well-informed about the United States.
  John Bartlet Brebner, 1895–1957, Canadian author and
  historian

Condoleezza Rice is apparently dating a Canadian politician. It's a proud day for Canada. They're the first nation to put a man on Condoleezza.
  David Letterman, 2006

(Canadians) better hope the United States does not roll over one night and crush them. They are lucky we allow them to exist on the same continent.
  Ann Coulter, American commentator and controversialist,
  Fox News, 2004

Canada could have enjoyed:
English government,
French culture,
and American know-how.
Instead it ended up with:
English know-how,
French government,
and American culture.
  John Robert Colombo, 'Oh Canada', 1965

Canada must be considered the Vichyssoise of nations – cold, half-French, and difficult to stir.
  Stuart Keate, Canadian newspaper publisher, 1913–87

An optimist in Canada is someone who thinks things could be worse.
  Preston Manning, Canadian politician

I'm not an American! I am a Canadian. I come from a 'nice', thoroughly unrealistic country.
  Matthew Fisher, Canadian journalist

Canadians have been so busy explaining to the Americans that we aren't British, and to the British that we aren't Americans that we haven't had time to become Canadians.
   Helen Gordon McPherson, Canadian author and speaker

The beaver, which has come to represent Canada as the eagle does the United States and the lion Britain, is a flat-tailed, slow-witted, toothy rodent known to bite off its own testicles or to stand under its own falling trees.
   June Callwood, 1924–2007, Canadian journalist and
   social activist

The US is our trading partner, our neighbour, our ally and our friend ... and sometimes we'd like to give them such a smack!
   Rick Mercer, Canadian blogger and political satirist

Canadians do not like heroes and so they do not have them.
   George Woodcock, 1912–95, *Canada and the Canadians*,
   1970

A Canadian is somebody who knows how to make love in a canoe.
   Pierre Berton, 1920–2004, Canadian commentator, *The
   Canadian*, 1973

Canada is a country whose main exports are hockey players and cold fronts. Our main imports are baseball players and acid rain.
   Pierre Elliott Trudeau, 1919–2000, 15th Prime Minister of
   Canada, 1968–79, 1980–84

If you want to see me again, don't bring signs saying 'Trudeau is a pig' and don't bring signs that he hustles women, because I won't talk to you. I didn't get into politics to be insulted. And don't throw wheat at me either. If you don't stop that, I'll kick you right in the ass.

Pierre Elliott Trudeau, addressing a young protester throwing wheat at him during a speech in Regina, 1969

Kate (to the Canadian ambassador): Ambassador, listen carefully. An hour ago I reviewed the United States' contingency plan to invade your country.
Will: Uh ... there's a contingency plan ...?
Kate: 1789, amended in 1815, the calligraphy is beautiful.

Carol Flint, *The West Wing*, 2005

#CANDIDATES

One of the great mysteries of politics is how a candidate can throw his hat in the ring and yet keep talking through it.

Sally Poplin, English humorous writer

When you think about it, it's unfair to hold people to what they say when they're madly in love, drunk or trying to get elected.

Anon.

A successful candidate is someone who can get into the public eye without irritating it.

Anon.

There are two sides to every question. And a good candidate takes both.

Anon.

Often in choosing a candidate, you go for the one who will do least harm.
Anon.

There are two types of candidate; the appointed and the disappointed.
Anon.

A candidate has a hard life. He has to shave twice a day.
Adlai Stevenson, 1900–65, Governor of Illinois,
Democratic Presidential Candidate 1952 and 1956

The politician is an acrobat. He keeps his balance by saying the opposite of what he does.
Maurice Barrès, 1862–1923, French journalist, novelist and socialist politician

... the hardest thing about an election campaign is how to win without proving that you are unworthy of winning.
Adlai Stevenson

Any man with a fine shock of hair, a good set of teeth and a bewitching smile, can park his brains, if he has any, and run for public office.
Franklin Dane, American wit

The more I see of the representatives of the people, the more I admire my dogs.
Alphonse de Lamartine, 1790–1869, French romantic poet and, briefly, Foreign Minister in 1848

It is dangerous for a candidate to say things that people might remember.

    Eugene McCarthy, 1916–2005, American poet, politician
    and Presidential hopeful, 1976

If you have a weak candidate and a weak platform, wrap yourself up in the American flag and talk about the Constitution.

    Matthew S. Quay, 1833–1904, Republican Senator, 1886

Elections are won by men and women chiefly because most people vote against somebody rather than for somebody.

    Franklin P. Adams, 1881–1960, American wit

See also: CAMPAIGNING, DEMOCRACY, ELECTIONS, MAJORITY, VOTING

#CAPITALISM

Capitalism without bankruptcy is like Christianity without hell.

    Frank Borman, NASA astronaut

A major source of objection to a free economy is precisely that it ... gives people what they want instead of what a particular group thinks they ought to want.

    Milton Friedman, 1912–2006, American economist,
    Capitalism and Freedom, 1962

Blake [William Blake, poet and painter] was not a politician, but there is more understanding of the nature of capitalist society in a poem like 'I wander through each charter'd street' than in three-quarters of Socialist literature.

George Orwell, 1903–50, *Dickens*, 1939

The fundamentals of capitalist ethics require that, 'You shall earn your bread in sweat' – unless you happen to have private means.

Michał Kalecki, 1899–1970, Polish economist, *Political Aspects of Full Employment*, 1943

Isn't capitalism wonderful? Under what other system could the ordinary man in the street owe so much?

Anon.

The trouble with the profit system has always been that it was highly unprofitable to most people.

E. B. White, *One Man's Meat*, 1944

Capitalism is what people do if you leave them alone.

Kenneth Minogue, Australian professor of political science

Depressing how capitalism took the quaint May Day tradition of village maidens skipping round the Maypole – and turned it into pole dancing.

John O'Farrell, British journalist, tweet, 2012

One of the criticisms levelled against capitalism is that it rewards the most ruthless and narcissistic: to which the only response is 'What? And politics doesn't?'

Ragingnick, posted on samizdata.net, 2011

RT '@petertatchell: 800 million people have no safe, clean drinking water. Capitalism has failed the world.' They do in capitalist countries.
Tom Greeves, tweet, October 2011

See also: CONSERVATIVE PARTY, CONSERVATIVES, LIBERALS V. CONSERVATIVES, LIBERTARIANISM, REPUBLICAN PARTY, REPUBLICAN SLOGANS, REPUBLICANS, LEFT V. RIGHT, TEA PARTY

#CARTER, JIMMY, 39TH PRESIDENT OF THE UNITED STATES, 1977–81

I would not want Jimmy Carter and his men put in charge of snake control in Ireland.
Eugene McCarthy

Jimmy Carter is a great ex-President. It's a shame he couldn't have gone directly to the ex-Presidency.
Thomas Mann, Brookings Institution Congressional scholar, 1994

My esteem in this country has gone up substantially. It is very nice now when people wave at me, they use all their fingers.
Jimmy Carter, after retirement

Jimmy Carter's basic problem is that he is super-cautious. He looks before – and after – he leaps.
Joey Adams, 1911–99, American comedian

He is your typical smiling, brilliant, back-stabbing, bullshitting southern nut-cutter.
   Lane Kirkland, 1922–99, US labor union leader

Sometimes I look at Billy and Jimmy and I say to myself, 'Lilian, you should have stayed a virgin.'
   Lilian Carter, of her two sons

I think Jimmy Carter as President is like Truman Capote marrying Dolly Parton. The job is just too big for him.
   Rich Little, American comedian (attrib.)

I don't know what people have against Jimmy Carter. He's done nothing.
   Bob Hope, 1903–2003, American comedian, campaigning
   for Ronald Reagan against Carter, 1980

See also: PRESIDENCY, WHITE HOUSE

#CHAMBERLAIN, NEVILLE, 1869–1940, CONSERVATIVE PRIME MINISTER, 1937–40

The worst thing I can say about democracy is that it has tolerated the right honourable gentleman for four and a half years.
   Aneurin Bevan, 1897–1960, Welsh Labour politician,
   speech in House of Commons

He has the lucidity which is the by-product of a fundamentally sterile mind.
   Aneurin Bevan

Mr Chamberlain views everything through the wrong end
of a municipal drain-pipe.
    David Lloyd George, 1863–1945, Liberal Prime Minister,
    1916–22 (attrib.) (Also attributed to Winston Churchill)

... a retail mind in a wholesale business.
    David Lloyd George

He might make an adequate Lord Mayor of Birmingham
in a lean year.
    David Lloyd George

Monsieur J'aime Berlin (Mr I-Love-Berlin)
    French nickname for Chamberlain (punning on the sound
    of 'Chamberlain' in French)

He looked less like a banana than an umbrella.
    Maurice Bowra, 1898–1971, British academic

Listening to a speech by Chamberlain is like paying a visit
to Woolworth's. Everything in its place and nothing above
sixpence.
    Aneurin Bevan, speech, House of Commons, 1937

... the mind and manner of a clothes brush.
    Harold Nicolson, 1886–1968, English author, 1938

See also: CONSERVATIVES, CONSERVATIVE PARTY

#CHURCHILL, SIR WINSTON, 1874-1965, WRITER, ORATOR AND BRITISH CONSERVATIVE POLITICIAN AND PRIME MINISTER, 1940-45, 1951-55

We are all worms, but I do believe that I am a glow-worm.
  Winston Churchill

I am easily satisfied with the very best.
  Winston Churchill, during the Second World War

The trouble with Winston is that he nails his trousers to the mast and can't climb down.
  Clement Attlee, 1883–1967, Labour Prime Minister
  1945–51

He refers to a defeat as if it came from God, but a victory as if it came from himself.
  Aneurin Bevan, speech in House of Commons, 1942

He is a man suffering from petrified adolescence.
  Aneurin Bevan

The mediocrity of his thinking is concealed by the majesty of his language.
  Aneurin Bevan (attrib.)

His ear is so sensitively attuned to the bugle note of history that he is often deaf to the more raucous clamour of modern life.
  Aneurin Bevan

Winston has devoted the best years of his life to preparing his impromptu speeches.
   F. E. Smith, 1st Earl of Birkenhead, 1872–1930, lawyer, orator, Conservative statesman (attrib.)

Bessie Braddock: Winston, you're drunk!
Churchill: Bessie, you're ugly. But tomorrow I shall be sober.
   Winston Churchill, probably apocryphal

Lady Astor: If you were my husband, I'd poison your coffee.
Churchill: If you were my wife, I'd drink it.
   Winston Churchill, at Blenheim Palace, 1912; probably apocryphal

See also: CONSERVATIVE PARTY, CONSERVATIVES

#CIVIL SERVICE AND WHITEHALL

(Whitehall) will create business for itself surely as a new railway will create traffic.
   Lord Salisbury, 1830–1903, Conservative statesman and three times Prime Minister, quoted in Andrew Roberts's *Salisbury: Victorian Titan*, 1999

... a difficulty for every solution.
   Lord Samuel, 1870–1963, Home Secretary, 1916 and 1931–32, of the civil service

The besetting sin of civil servants is to mix too much with each other.
   Sir William Beveridge, 1879–1963, British economist and social reformer, Director of the London School of Economics, 1924

If there is anything a public servant hates to do, it's something for the public.
Anon.

The first forty-eight hours decide whether a minister is going to run his office or whether his office is going to run him.
Arthur Henderson, 1863–1935, Labour MP and three times leader of the Labour Party

There are occasions when you have to say 'bollocks' to ministers.
Sir Richard Wilson, Secretary of the Cabinet and Head of the Home Civil Service from 1998

We dare not allow politicians to establish the principle that senior civil servants can be removed for incompetence. We could lose dozens of our chaps. Hundreds maybe. Even thousands.
Antony Jay and Jonathan Lynn, *Yes Minister*, 1986

The opposition aren't really the opposition. They are only the government in exile. The civil service are the opposition in residence.
Antony Jay and Jonathan Lynn, *Yes Minister*, 1980

Too much civil service work consists of circulating information that isn't relevant about subjects that don't matter to people who aren't interested.
Antony Jay and Jonathan Lynn, *Yes Minister*, Preface

We're all fucked. I'm fucked. You're fucked. The whole
department's fucked. It's been the biggest cock-up ever and
we're all completely fucked.

> Sir Richard Mottram, former Permanent Secretary at the
> Department of Transport, February 2002, about a scandal-
> ous email

See also: BUREAUCRACY, GOVERNMENT, LOCAL
GOVERNMENT

#CLINTON, BILL, 42ND PRESIDENT OF THE UNITED STATES, 1993–2001

An official Gallup survey polled over 1,000 women with
the question: Would you sleep with Bill Clinton?
1 per cent said, 'No'
2 per cent said, 'Yes'
97 per cent said, 'Never Again'

> Anon.

The other day while playing golf in England, President
Clinton met a couple getting married and posed for pictures
with them. Not only that but he offered to help consummate the marriage.

> Conan O'Brien, late-night talk-show host, 2001

Bill Clinton's foreign policy achievements are pretty much
confined to having had breakfast once at the International
House of Pancakes.

> Pat Buchanan, American conservative commentator

Bill Clinton is a man who thinks international affairs means dating a girl from out of town.
Tom Clancy, American novelist

... a hard dog to keep on the porch.
Hillary Clinton, *Talk*, 1999

I think most of us learned a long time ago that if you don't like the President's position on a particular issue, you simply need to wait a few weeks.
David Obey, Democratic Congressman

I think President Clinton misunderstood the role of the President, which is to screw the country as a whole, not individually.
Betsy Salkind, American comedian

President Clinton apparently gets so much action that every couple of weeks they have to spray WD-40 on his zipper.
David Letterman

He's going around the country ... basically thanking himself for being our President.
Chris Matthews, MSNBC commentator, on Clinton's farewell tour, 2000

My dog Millie knows more about foreign affairs than these two bozos.
George W. Bush, 43rd President of the United States, 2001–09, referring to Clinton and Gore, 1992 (attrib.)

If Bill Clinton was Moses, he would have come down with the Ten Suggestions.
Bill Maher, *Politically Incorrect*, 1993

You know, the clock is running down on the Republicans in Congress, too. I feel for them, I do. They've only got seven more months to investigate me. That's a lot of pressure. So little time, so many unanswered questions.

For example, over the last few months I've lost ten pounds. Where did they go? Why haven't I produced them to the independent counsel?

Bill Clinton, farewell speech to White House
Correspondents' Dinner, 2000

Now some of you might think I've been busy writing my memoirs. I'm not concerned about my memoirs, I'm concerned about my resumé.

Here's what I've got so far: Career Objective – to stay President.

But being realistic I would consider an executive position with another country. 'Course, I'd prefer to stay within the G8.

Bill Clinton, farewell speech to White House
Correspondents' Dinner, 2000

They tell me I have to use the active voice for the resumé. You know, things like, '*Commanded* US armed forces. *Ordered* air strikes. *Served* three times as President.' Everybody embellishes a little!

Bill Clinton, farewell speech to White House
Correspondents' Dinner, 2000

Former President Clinton, now that he's out of office he has to make his money like all the rest of us. This week kicks off the big public speaking tour, and he's down there in Florida ... doing two speeches and judging a wet T-shirt contest.

David Letterman, 2002

See also: PRESIDENCY, WHITE HOUSE

#COMMUNISM

What is a communist? One who hath yearnings
For equal division of unequal earnings,
Idler or bungler, or both, he is willing
To fork out his copper and pocket your shilling.
  Ebenezer Elliott, 1781–1849, epigram, 1850

Communism might be likened to a race in which all competitors come in first with no prizes.
  Lord Inchcape, 1852–1932, British businessman and colonial administrator, quoted in *The Observer*, 1924

The colour of communism was not red but grey.
  Richard Nixon, 1913–94, 37th President of the United States, 1969–74

When I see a bird that talks like a duck and swims like a duck and quacks like a duck, I call it a duck.
  Walter Reuther, 1907–70, American union leader, on spotting a communist (attrib.)

Nature has no cure for this sort of madness, though I know a legacy from a rich relative works wonders.
  F. E. Smith, on Bolshevism, *Law, Life and Letters*, 1927

A Communist is someone who has nothing and wishes to share it with the world.
  Anon.

Any man who is not a Communist at the age of twenty is a fool. Any man who is still a Communist at the age of thirty is an even bigger fool.
  George Bernard Shaw, 1856–1950, Irish playwright

Communism is like Prohibition, it's a good idea but it won't work.
    Will Rogers, 1879–1935, American commentator and
    humorist, *The Autobiography of Will Rogers*, 1949

These were people who believed everything about the Soviet Union was perfect, but they were bringing their own toilet paper.
    P. J. O'Rourke, *Republican Party Reptile*, 1987

A Communist is a socialist without a sense of humour.
    George Cutton, American wit

Communism doesn't work because people like to own stuff.
    Frank Zappa, 1940–93, composer and rock musician

Communism was a great system for making people equally poor. In fact, there was no better system in the world for that than communism.
    Thomas L. Friedman, *The World is Flat*, 2005

The Marxist law of distribution of wealth is that shortages will be divided equally among the peasants.
    John Guftason, American wit

No member of our generation who wasn't a Communist or a dropout in the thirties is worth a damn.
    Lyndon B. Johnson, 1908–73, 36th President of the United
    States, 1963–69 (attrib.)

How do you tell a Communist? Well, it's someone who reads Marx and Lenin.

And how do you tell an anti-Communist?

It's someone who understands Marx and Lenin.

> Ronald Reagan, 1911–2004, 40th President of the United
> States, 1981–89 (attrib.)

Send your son to Moscow and he will return an anti-Communist; send him to the Sorbonne and he will return a Communist.

> Félix Houphouët-Boigny, 1905–73, First President of the
> Ivory Coast

In the end we beat them with Levi 501 jeans. Seventy-two years of Communist indoctrination and propaganda was drowned out by a three-ounce Sony Walkman. A huge totalitarian system ... has been brought to its knees because nobody wants to wear Bulgarian shoes ... Now they're lunch and we're number one on the planet.

> P. J. O'Rourke, 'The Death of Communism', *Rolling Stone*,
> 1989

Communism doesn't really starve or execute that many people. Mainly it just bores them to death.

> P. J. O'Rourke, *Holidays in Hell*, 1989

I've been to your Communist countries. They are crap-your-pants-ugly, dull-as-church, dead-from-the-dick-up places where government is to life what panty hose are to sex.

> P. J. O'Rourke, *Holidays in Hell*, 1989

You can't get good Chinese takeout in China and Cuban cigars are rationed in Cuba. That's all you need to know about Communism.
P. J. O'Rourke, *Give War a Chance*, 1992

Wherever there is a jackboot stomping on a human face there will be a well-heeled Western liberal to explain that the face does, after all, enjoy free health care and 100 per cent literacy.
John Derbyshire, British-American writer, journalist and commentator

There is not one single social or economic principle or concept in the philosophy of the Russian Bolshevik which has not been realised, carried into action and enshrined in immutable laws a million years ago by the white ant.
Winston Churchill, 'Politics', *The Churchill Wit*, 1965

The objection to a Communist always resolves itself into the fact that he is not a gentleman.
H. L. Mencken, 1880–1956, *Minority Report*, 1956

Totalitarian systems of government and totalitarian ideologies have a single source, which is resentment.
Roger Scruton, English philosopher

Australian Communists are pathological exhibits, human scum, paranoiacs, degenerates, morons, bludgers, pack of dingoes, industrial outlaws and political lepers, ratbags. If these people went to Russia, Stalin wouldn't even use them for manure.
Arthur Calwell, 1896–1973, politician and Leader of the Australian Labor Party, 1960–67

Communism Killed 100 Million People and All I Got Was
This Lousy T-Shirt
   Slogan on Che Guevara T-shirt

A man's admiration for absolute government is proportion-
ate to the contempt he feels for those around him.
   Alexis de Tocqueville, 1805–1859, French political thinker
   and historian

See also: CUBA, DEMOCRAT SLOGANS,
DEMOCRATIC PARTY, DEMOCRATS V.
REPUBLICANS, DEMOCRATS, EQUALITY,
LABOUR PARTY, LEFT V. RIGHT, LEFT, LIBERAL
PARTY, LIBERALS AND LIBERALISM, LIBERALS
V. CONSERVATIVES, NORTH KOREA, MARXISM,
SOCIALISM V. CAPITALISM, SOCIALISM

#CONGRESS

Congress is so strange. A man gets up to speak and says
nothing. Nobody listens – and then everybody disagrees.
   Boris Marshalov, 1902–67, Russian writer, after a visit to
   the House of Representatives

Reader, suppose you were an idiot. And suppose you were
a member of Congress. But I repeat myself.
   Mark Twain, 1835–1910, American writer and humorist

It could probably be shown by facts and figures that there
is no distinctly native American criminal class except
Congress.
   Mark Twain, *Following the Equator*, 1897

You can't use tact with a Congressman. A Congressman is a hog. You must take a stick and hit him on the snout.
Henry Adams, 1838–1918, American journalist, novelist and historian

We have the power to do any damn fool thing we want to do and we seem to do it about every ten minutes.
William Fulbright, 1905–95, Senator representing Arkansas, 1945–75

You can lead a man to Congress but you can't make him think.
Milton Berle, 1908–2002, American comedian

Senate office hours are from twelve to one with an hour off for lunch.
George S. Kaufman, 1889–1961, American playwright

Donna: Schadenfreude?
C. J.: You know, enjoying the suffering of others. The whole rationale behind the House of Representatives.
Alexa Junge, *The West Wing*, 2003

The members of Congress never open their mouths without subtracting from the sum of human knowledge.
Thomas Reed, 1839–1902, speaker of the House of Representatives, 1889–91 and 1895–99

I've had a tough time learning how to be a Congressman. Today I accidentally spent some of my own money.
Joseph P. Kennedy II, American businessman and Democratic politician

In my many years I have come to a conclusion that one useless man is a shame, two is a law firm, and three or more is a congress.

John Adams, 1735–1826, 2nd President of the United States, 1797–1801

This country has come to feel the same when Congress is in session as we do when the baby gets hold of the hammer. It's just a question of how much damage he can do with it before we can take it away from him.

Will Rogers, quoted in *Will Rogers: His Life and Times*, 1973

Congress does from a third to half of what I think is the minimum that it ought to do, and I am profoundly grateful that I get as much.

Theodore Roosevelt, 1858–1919, 26th President of the United States, 1901–09

Leo: Even when they're here in session, getting a hundred senators in line is still like trying to get cats to walk in a parade.

Aaron Sorkin, *The West Wing*, 2000

See also: WASHINGTON

#CONSERVATIVE PARTY, THE

It is a bizarre biological fact that the Conservative Party can be directed along a sensible left-wing path only by a leader with impeccable aristocratic connections.

Humphrey Berkeley, 1926–94, Conservative MP, of Conservative Prime Minister Harold Macmillan

The Conservative Party is an organised hypocrisy.
  Benjamin Disraeli, speech in the House of Commons, 1845

The trouble with the Conservative Party is that it has not
turned the clock back a single second.
  Evelyn Waugh, 1903–66, English novelist (attrib.)

There is nothing that so improves the mood of the Party
than the imminent execution of a senior colleague.
  Alan Clark, 1928–99, British Conservative MP, *Diary*, 1990

If capitalism depended on the intellectual quality of the
Conservative Party, it would end about lunchtime tomorrow.
  Tony Benn, Labour MP

The Conservative Party always in time forgives those
who were wrong. Indeed often, in time, they forgive
those who were right.
  Iain Macleod, 1913–70, Conservative Cabinet minister

Growing older, I have lost the need to be political, which
means, in this country, the need to be left. I am driven into
grudging toleration of the Conservative Party because it is
the party of non-politics, of resistance to politics.
  Kingsley Amis, 1922–95, English poet and novelist

The Conservative Party has never believed that the business
of the government is the government of business.
  Nigel Lawson, Conservative politician and journalist

The Tory Party never panics, except in a crisis.
  Sir John Hoskyns, policy advisor to Margaret Thatcher

The Tory Party are the cream of England: rich, thick and full of clots.

Sally Poplin

As another Tory boasted to me recently, 'If there's one thing we're really good at in this party, it's knifing our failing leaders in the back.'

James Delingpole, *Daily Telegraph*, 2012

See also: CAPITALISM, CONSERVATIVES, LIBERALS V. CONSERVATIVES, LIBERTARIANISM, REPUBLICAN PARTY, REPUBLICAN SLOGANS, REPUBLICANS, LEFT V. RIGHT, TEA PARTY

#CONSERVATIVES AND CONSERVATISM

In 1904, 20 per cent of journeys were made by bicycle in London. I want to see a figure like that again. If you can't turn the clock back to 1904, what's the point of being a Conservative?

Boris Johnson, Conservative Mayor of London, launching a bike hire scheme, 2010

It seems to me a barren thing, this Conservatism – an unhappy cross-breed, the mule of politics that engenders nothing.

Benjamin Disraeli, 1804–81, writer and Conservative Prime Minister, 1874–80

When a nation's young men are conservative, its funeral bell is already rung.

Henry Ward Beecher, 1813–87, *Proverbs from Plymouth Pulpit*, 1887

A conservative is a man who will not look at the new moon out of respect for that ancient institution, the old one.

  Douglas Jerrold, 1803–57, English dramatist and writer

No man can become a conservative until he has something to lose.

  James P. Warburg, 1896–1969, American banker and advisor
  to Franklin D. Roosevelt

Traditionalists are pessimists about the future and optimists about the past.

  Lewis Mumford, 1895–1990, American historian and critic

Conservative, n. A statesman who is enamoured of existing evils, as distinguished from the Liberal, who wishes to replace them with others.

  Ambrose Bierce, 1842–1913, *The Devil's Dictionary*, 1911

A conservative is a man who does not believe anything should be done for the first time.

  Frank A. Vanderlip, 1864–1937, American banker

Orthodoxy: That peculiar condition where the patient can neither eliminate an old idea nor absorb a new one.

  Elbert Hubbard, 1856–1915, *The Note Book of Elbert Hubbard*, 1927

Men who are orthodox when they are young are in danger of being middle-aged all their lives.

  Walter Lippmann, 1889–1974, American intellectual,
  writer and political commentator

A conservative is a man who is too cowardly to fight and too fat to run.
Elbert Hubbard, *The Note Book of Elbert Hubbard*, 1927

The modern conservative is engaged in one of man's oldest exercises in moral philosophy, that is the search for a superior moral justification for selfishness.
John Kenneth Galbraith, 1908–2006, Canadian-American economist

A conservative is someone who demands a square deal for the rich.
Sally Poplin

The only difference between a rut and a grave are their dimensions.
Ellen Glasgow, 1873–1945, American novelist

Once you leave the womb, conservatives don't care about you until you reach military age. Then you're just what they're looking for.
George Carlin, 1937–2008, American comedian

I'd rather be a conservative nut job
Than a liberal with no nuts and no job.
T-shirt, Washington, 2010

Tories are not always wrong, but they are always wrong at the right moment.
Lady Violet Bonham-Carter, 1915–53, Liberal politician

Of course no one likes the Conservatives. They only vote for us because they think we are right.
Peter Lilley, Conservative Cabinet minister

The Conservative establishment has always treated women as nannies, grannies and fannies.

Teresa Gorman, Conservative MP 1987–2001

They are nothing else but a load of kippers – two-faced, with no guts.

Eric Heffer, 1922–91, Labour MP (attrib.)

I was born in Rotherham. Around where I lived, people thought a Conservative was something you spread on your toast.

William Hague, Conservative Party leader 1997–2001, quoted in *The Guardian*, 1997

Conservatives do not believe that political struggle is the most important thing in life. The simplest among them prefer fox hunting, the wisest, religion.

Quintin Hogg, 1907–2001, *The Case for Conservatism*, 1947

See also: CAPITALISM, CONSERVATIVE PARTY, FASCISM, LIBERALS V. CONSERVATIVES, LIBERTARIANISM, REPUBLICAN PARTY, REPUBLICAN SLOGANS, REPUBLICANS, LEFT V. RIGHT, TEA PARTY

#CONSERVATIVES V. LIBERALS

See: LIBERALS V. CONSERVATIVES

#COOLIDGE, CALVIN, 1872-1933, 30TH PRESIDENT OF THE UNITED STATES, 1923-29

Democracy is that system of government under which the people, having 35,717,342 native-born adult whites to choose from, including thousands who are handsome and many of whom are wise, pick out Coolidge to be head of state.
  H. L. Mencken

No man ever listened himself out of a job.
  Calvin Coolidge

I do wish he didn't look as if he had been weaned on a pickle.
  Alice Roosevelt Longworth, 1884–1980, oldest child of
  Theodore Roosevelt

How could they tell?
  Dorothy Parker, 1893–1967, American poet and satirist,
  after being told of Coolidge's death

Mr Coolidge's genius for inactivity is developed to a very high point. It is far from being an indolent activity. It is a grim, determined, alert inactivity which keeps Mr Coolidge occupied constantly ... Inactivity is a political philosophy and a party program with Mr Coolidge.
  Walter Lippmann, *Men of Destiny,* 1927

... simply a cheap and trashy fellow, deficient in sense and almost devoid of any notion of honor – in brief, a dreadful little cad.
  H. L. Mencken, *Baltimore Evening Sun,* 1924

He is the first President to discover that what the American people want is to be left alone.
Will Rogers, newspaper column, 1924

He slept more than any other President, whether by day or by night. Nero fiddled but Coolidge only snored.
H .L. Mencken, *American Mercury*, 1933

See also: PRESIDENCY, WHITE HOUSE

#CORRUPTION

The illegal we do immediately. The unconstitutional takes a little longer.
Henry Kissinger, American diplomat

An honest politician is one who, when he is bought, will stay bought.
Simon Cameron, 1799–1889, Secretary of War under Abraham Lincoln

I have often been accused of putting my foot in my mouth, but I will never put my hand in your pockets.
Spiro Agnew, 1918–96, 39th Vice President of the United States, 1969–73

Few men have virtue to withstand the highest bidder.
George Washington, 1732–99, 1st President of the United States, 1789–97

#CREDIT CRUNCH

A recession is when your neighbour loses his job. A depression is when you lose yours. And a recovery is when Jimmy Carter loses his.
Ronald Reagan, electioneering, 1980

Yes, [Secretary of the Treasury] Hank Paulson believes the economy is now on a solid foundation. I think he means it's on the rocks.
Anon.

A deficit is what you have when you haven't as much as you had when you had nothing.
Anon.

The economy hasn't reached rock-bottom yet – but if we keep climbing, it soon will.
Anon.

Will the dollar be even weaker under another Republican government?
Yes, that's the $24,000 Question.
Anon.

I'm worried – did you see that [Secretary of the Treasury] Hank Paulson said yesterday that things are going to get a lot worse before they get worse.
Anon.

I'm haunted by two worries: first, will we ever get back to the good old days? And secondly, these may be them.
Anon.

We're now at the bridge we were going to cross when we came to it.
  Anon.

See also: BANKS AND BANKING, BIG BUSINESS, BUSINESS, CAPITALISM, ECONOMICS AND ECONOMISTS, ECONOMY, INFLATION, MONEY, POVERTY, RICH AND POOR, STOCK MARKET AND WALL STREET, TAXATION, WEALTH

#CUBA

We're eyeball to eyeball and I think the other fellow just blinked.
  Dean Rusk, 1909–94, US Secretary of State 1961–69, on
  the Cuban Missile Crisis, 1962

Miami's Hispanic population took to the streets last night to celebrate Fidel Castro temporarily stepping down from power. Way to go America! Our plan to slowly deteriorate his health over the course of fifty years is working.
  Stephen Colbert, *The Colbert Report*, Comedy Central,
  2006

Cuban dictator Fidel Castro is still in the hospital with a serious medical condition. Castro said that a half-century of Communist rule seemed like a good idea right up until the point he was rushed to the hospital in a '55 Oldsmobile.
  Conan O'Brien, 2006

He ran Cuba for almost fifty years. And political analysts are now debating what kind of changes the Cuban people will hope for. I'm gonna guess: term limits.

Jay Leno, late-night talk-show host, 2006

In a speech in Florida President Bush praised all the contributions Cubans have made to America: catching, hitting, outfielding, shortstop. These were all major, major contributions.

Jay Leno, 2006

See also: COMMUNISM, MARXISM, NORTH KOREA, SOCIALISM

D

#DEATH PENALTY

I'm for a stronger death penalty.
    George H. W. Bush, 41st President of the United States, 1989–93

When I came back to Dublin, I was court-martialled in my absence and sentenced to death in my absence, so I said they could shoot me in my absence.
    Brendan Behan, *The Hostage*, 1959

Why Do We Kill People Who Kill People To Show That Killing People Is Wrong?
    T-shirt slogan, Florida 2000

See also: JUSTICE, LAW

#DEBATE

It is difficult to get a man to understand something when his salary depends upon him not understanding it.
    Upton Sinclair, 1878–1968, American author

If you can find something everyone agrees on, it's wrong.
    Mo Udall, 1922–98, Democratic politician

When political ammunition runs low, inevitably the rusty artillery of abuse is always wheeled into action.

> Adlai Stevenson, 1900–1965, Governor of Illinois,
> Democratic Presidential candidate 1952 and 1956,
> speech, New York City, 1952

One of the most curious things about American politics is that, without a single historical exception, a partisan is invariably a member of the other party.

> Anon.

Once you've taken a public stand you know is right, never back down; anything less than a rock-hard stance will let your enemies nibble you to death.

> L. Neil Smith, libertarian author and political activist

Leo: We're not going to stop, soften, detour, postpone, circumvent, obfuscate or trade a single one of our goals to allow for whatever extracurricular nonsense is coming our way in the next days, weeks and months.
Toby: When did we decide this?
Leo: Just now.

> Aaron Sorkin, *The West Wing*, 2001

Win every argument simply by repeating your opponent's last sentence in a whiny voice.

> Twop Twips, tweet, 2012

Rebellion is like adultery... It's a big thing the first time. Later it becomes a bit easier, perhaps even ends up as a habit.

> Anonymous Conservative minister, quoted by Martin Kettle,
> *The Guardian*, 2012

That one never asks a question unless one knows the answer is basic to parliamentary questioning.

> John Diefenbaker, 1895–1979, 13th Prime Minister of Canada, 1957–63

See also: CONGRESS, HOUSE OF COMMONS, HOUSE OF LORDS

#DEFENCE

Josh: Ten words: 'I will make America's defences the strongest in the history of the world.'
Leo: 'In the history of the world?' When we say that, are we comparing ourselves to the Visigoths, adjusted for inflation?

> Aaron Sorkin and Paul Redford, *The West Wing*, 2002

Department of Defense: We kill people – so you don't have to!

> Anon.

See also: ARMY, MILITARY, WAR

#DEMOCRACY

A majority is always the best repartee.

> Benjamin Disraeli, 1804–81, *Tancred*, 1847

Democracy is two wolves and a lamb voting on what to have for lunch.

> Anon.

Democracy is the recurrent suspicion that more than half of the people are right more than half of the time.
     E. B. White, 1899–1985, *New Yorker*, 1944

Democracy means government by discussion, but it is only effective if you can stop people talking.
     Clement Attlee, 1883–1967, Labour Prime Minister,
     1945–51, speech at Oxford, 1957

Democracy is ... a form of religion; it is the worship of jackals by jackasses.
     H. L. Mencken, 1880–1956, *Sententiae*, 1920

Democracy is the art of running the circus from the monkey cage.
     H. L. Mencken

Two cheers for Democracy: one because it admits variety and two because it permits criticism. Two cheers are quite enough: there is no occasion to give three.
     E. M. Forster, 1879–1970, English novelist and essayist,
     Two Cheers for Democracy, 1951

Democracy gives every man the right to be his own oppressor.
     James Russell Lowell, 1819–91, American poet, critic
     and diplomat

DEMOCRACY IS TOO GOOD TO SHARE WITH JUST ANYBODY
     Graffito

Democracy is a government of bullies tempered by editors.
     Ralph Waldo Emerson, 1803–82, American essayist,
     lecturer and poet

Democracy is a form of government by popular ignorance.
   Elbert Hubbard, 1856–1915, American publisher, artist,
   essayist and poet

The best argument against democracy is a five-minute
conversation with the average voter.
   Winston Churchill, 1874–1965, British statesman, orator
   and writer

In democracy everyone has the right to be represented, even
the jerks.
   Chris Patten, Conservative politician and administrator

The great thing about living in a democracy is that you can
say what you think without thinking.
   Dwight D. Eisenhower, 1890–1969, 34th American
   President, 1953–61

One fifth of the people are against everything all the time.
   Robert F. Kennedy, 1925–68, American politician,
   Democratic Senator and civil rights activist

Democracy is simply the bludgeoning of the people by the
people for the people.
   Oscar Wilde, 1854–1900, Irish playwright

Democracy is the theory that the common people know
what they want, and deserve to get it good and hard.
   H. L. Mencken, *A Book of Burlesques*, 1920

Many forms of government have been tried, and will be tried in this world of sin and woe. No one pretends that democracy is perfect or all-wise. Indeed, it has been said that democracy is the worst form of government except all those other forms that have been tried from time to time.

Winston Churchill, speech, House of Commons, 1947

Democracy is a device that insures we shall be governed no better than we deserve.

George Bernard Shaw, 1856–1950, Irish playwright

In contrast to totalitarianism, democracy can face and live with the truth about itself.

Sidney Hook, 1902–89, American philosopher

Democracy is a pathetic belief in the collective wisdom of individual ignorance.

H. L. Mencken, American essayist and critic

I have great faith in the people; as for their wisdom – well, Coca-Cola still outsells champagne.

Adlai Stevenson, Democratic Presidential candidate
defeated by Eisenhower in 1952 and 1956

Democracy is welcoming people from other lands, and giving them something to hold on to – usually a mop or a leaf-blower.

Johnny Carson, American late-night TV host

You have to remember one thing about the will of the people: it wasn't that long ago that we were swept away by the Macarena.

Jon Stewart, *The Daily Show*, Comedy Central

See also: DICTATORSHIP, ELECTIONS, GOVERNMENT, VOTING

#DEMOCRAT SLOGANS

DEMOCRATS. CLEANING UP REPUBLICAN MESSES SINCE 1933.
  Bumper sticker, Los Angeles, 2008

DEMOCRATS ARE SEXY.
WHO EVER HEARD OF A NICE PIECE OF ELEPHANT?
  Bumper sticker, Florida, 2008

See also: THE DEMOCRATIC PARTY, DEMOCRATS, DEMOCRATS V. REPUBLICANS

#DEMOCRATIC PARTY, THE

The Democratic Party is like a man riding backwards in a carriage. It never sees a thing until it has gone by.
  Benjamin Butler, 1818–93, Republican Congressman
  and Governor

The Democratic Party at its worst is better for the country than the Republican Party at its best.
  Lyndon B. Johnson, 1908–73, 36th President of the United
  States, 1963–69

Thomas Jefferson founded the Democratic Party. Franklin Roosevelt dumbfounded it.
  Dewey Short, 1898–1979, Republican congressman

There were so many candidates on the Democratic plat-
form, there were not enough promises to go round.
  Ronald Reagan, 1911–2004, 40th President of the United
  States, 1981–89

The principal purpose of the Democratic Party is to use the
force of government to take property away from the people
who earn it and give it to people who do not.
  Neal Boortz, American radio host and political commentator

The Democratic Party is like a mule – without pride of
ancestry or hope of posterity.
  Edmund Burke, 1729–97, Irish political philosopher and
  statesman

The [Democratic] government's view of the economy could
be summed up in a few short phrases: If it moves, tax
it. If it keeps moving, regulate it. And if it stops moving,
subsidise it.
  Ronald Reagan, speech to small-businessmen, 1986

The room erupted in spontaneous applause, very similar
to what you hear at Democratic Party dinners when somebody mentions the poor.
  Dave Barry, *Miami Herald*

Serious Democrats need to confront the intellectual empti-
ness of their party, which Kerry's campaign embodies all
too well. The Dems got a full tank from FDR, a top-up
in the Civil Rights era, and they've been running on fumes
for thirty years.
  Mark Steyn, *Chicago Sun-Times*, 2004

See also: DEMOCRATS, DEMOCRAT SLOGANS

#DEMOCRATS

I sleep like a Democrat. I LIE on one side and then I LIE on the other!

    T-shirt slogan, Houston 2008

You Might Be A Democrat If ...

- You believe that a few hundred loggers can find another career, but the defenceless spotted owl must live in its preferred tree.
- You believe our government must do it because everyone in Europe does.
- You don't understand why anyone was bothered by Jane's trip to Hanoi.
- You think solar energy is being held back by those greedy oil companies.
- You've never been mugged.
- You think Ayn Rand is an African currency.
- Your high school yearbook goals included the words 'help people'.
- You think the free market is where they hand out government cheese.
- You know at least one vegan.
- You actually think that poverty can be abolished.
  Internet

You can never underestimate the ability of the Democrats to wet their finger and hold it to the wind.

    Ronald Reagan

You've got to be an optimist to be a Democrat and you've got to be a humorist to stay one.
  Will Rogers

I belong to no organised party – I am a Democrat.
  Will Rogers, 1879–1935, American commentator
  and humorist

The Democrats seem to be basically nicer people, but they have demonstrated time and again that they have the management skills of celery.
  Dave Barry, *Miami Herald*

A Democrat is just like a baby. If it's hollering and making a lot of noise, there is nothing serious the matter with it. When it's quiet and doesn't pay much attention to anything, that's when it's really dangerous.
  Will Rogers, *I Never Met a Man I Didn't Like*, 1991

See also: DEMOCRATIC PARTY, DEMOCRAT SLOGANS, DEMOCRATS V. REPUBLICANS

#DEMOCRATS V. REPUBLICANS

Republicans sleep in twin beds – some even in separate rooms. That is why there are more Democrats.
  Will Stanton, 1918–86, 'How to Tell a Democrat from a
  Republican', 1962

Republicans are very good at describing things in black and white; Democrats are very good at describing the eleven shades of grey.
  Joseph C. Wilson, American diplomat and consultant, 2005

Republicans raise dahlias, Dalmatians, and eyebrows.
Democrats raise Airedales, kids and taxes.
   Will Stanton

What Democratic congressmen do to their women staffers,
Republican congressmen do to the country.
   Bill Maher, late-night talk-show host

Compared to the Clintons, Reagan is living proof that a
Republican with half a brain is better than a Democrat
with two.
   P. J. O'Rourke, libertarian journalist and commentator

... while the Republicans are smart enough to make money,
the Democrats are smart enough to get in office every two
or three times a century and take it away from 'em.
   Will Rogers, radio talk, 1934

Democrats make up plans and then do something else.
Republicans follow the plans their grandfathers made
... Republican boys date Democratic girls. They plan to
marry Republican girls, but feel they're entitled to a little
fun first.
   Andrew Jacobs Jr, Democratic Congressman, House
   debate, 1983

Republicans study the financial pages of the newspaper.
Democrats put them in the bottom of the bird cage.
   Will Stanton

You have to have been a Republican to know how good it is to be a Democrat.
    Jackie Onassis, 1929–94, widow of John F. Kennedy

There is something about a Republican that you can only stand him for so long; and, on the other hand, there is something about a Democrat that you can't stand him for quite that long.
    Will Rogers

It seems to be a law of nature that Republicans are more boring than Democrats.
    Stewart Alsop, 1914–74, American columnist and political analyst

If Democrats Had Any Brains, They'd Be Republicans
    Ann Coulter, American commentator and controversialist, book title, 2007

I relate to both parties. I eat like an elephant and act like a jackass.
    Rich Little, American comedian, *Sunday Morning*, 1988

We need Democrats. They are on this world to distribute wealth. But we first need a party that can create the wealth to distribute.
    Jack F. Kemp, 1935–2009, Republican Congressman, 'Firing Line,' *PBS*, 1988

May you be as rich as a Republican and have the sex life of a Democrat.
    Johnny Carson

Josh: When voters want a national daddy ... someone to be tough and strong and defend the country, they vote Republican. When they want a mommy, someone to give them jobs, health care ... the policy equivalent of matzah-ball soup, they vote Democrat.

Eli Attie, *The West Wing*, 2005

I have only one firm belief about the American political system, and that is this: God is a Republican and Santa Claus is a Democrat.

P. J. O'Rourke, *Parliament of Whores*, 1991

Republicans have nothing but bad ideas and Democrats have no ideas.

Lewis Black, American stand-up comedian, author and playwright

President Bartlet: We agree on nothing, Max.

Senator Lobell: Yes, sir.

Bartlet: Education, guns, drugs, school prayer, gays, defence spending, taxes – you name it, we disagree.

Senator Lobell: You know why?

Bartlet: Because I'm a lily-livered, bleeding-heart, liberal, egghead communist.

Senator Lobell: Yes, sir. And I'm a gun-toting, redneck son-of-a-bitch.

Bartlet: Yes, you are.

Senator Lobell: We agree about that.

Aaron Sorkin, *The West Wing*, 2000

See also: DEMOCRAT SLOGANS, DEMOCRATIC PARTY, DEMOCRATS, LEFT V. RIGHT

#DEPARTURES

Galbraith's Law states that anyone who says he won't resign four times, will.
  John Kenneth Galbraith, 1908–2006, Canadian-American economist

I do believe politicians would be far more ready to resign office if they did not feel that their doing so would give such infinite pleasure to their adversaries.
  Lord Salisbury, 1830–1903, Conservative statesman and three times Prime Minister, letter 1889

I am now celebrating the twentieth anniversary of the first request for my resignation. I look forward to many more.
  Richard Darman, 1943–2008, American businessman and economist who served under five Presidents, chiefly George H. W. Bush

Like a glorious tropical sunset, a resigning politician is a beautiful sight.
  Matthew Parris, former Conservative MP, *The Times*, 1992

There's only one way to leave power and that's kicking and screaming.
  P. J. Mara, Irish PR advisor and former senator

Now I am no longer President, I find I no longer win every game of golf I play.
  George H. W. Bush

Nothing excites compassion, in friend and foe alike, as much as the sight of you ker-splonked on the Tarmac with your propeller buried six feet under.
Boris Johnson, *Daily Telegraph*, 2004, on being sacked from the Conservative front bench

My friends, as I have discovered myself, there are no disasters, only opportunities. And, indeed, opportunities for fresh disasters.
Boris Johnson, *Daily Telegraph*, 2004, on being sacked from the Conservative front bench

You realise you're no longer in government when you get in the back of your car and it doesn't go anywhere.
Malcolm Rifkind, former Conservative minister

In over fifty years of political life I have learned at least one valuable lesson: if anyone offers to resign in a huff, accept! It saves time.
Lord Beaumont of Whitley, 1928–2008, clergyman and Green Party peer

There is nothing so ex as an ex-MP.
Tam Dalyell, Scottish Labour MP and Father of the House of Commons, on his retirement

#DICTATORSHIP

As the saying goes, *1984* was supposed to be a warning, not a manual.
Anon.

Dictators are rulers who always look good until the last ten minutes.
 Jan Masaryk, 1886–1948, Czech diplomat

A dictatorship is a country where they have taken the politics out of politics.
 Sam Himmell, American wit

A dictatorship would be a heck of a lot easier, there's no question about it.
 George W. Bush, 43rd President of the United States, 2001–09

Dictators ride to and fro upon tigers which they dare not dismount. And the tigers are getting hungry.
 Winston Churchill

Dictatorship is like a great beech tree – nice to look at but nothing grows under it.
 Stanley Baldwin, 1867–1947, Conservative politician and three-time Prime Minister

See also: DEMOCRACY, TYRANTS

#DIPLOMACY

An ambassador is an honest man sent to lie abroad for the good of his country.
 Sir Henry Wotton, 1568–1639, British diplomat and poet

I have discovered the art of fooling diplomats: I speak the truth and they never believe me.
 Camillo di Cavour, 1810–61, Italian politician

If you consider the position of the Russians ethically, it is as bad as can be. Negotiating with them is like catching soaped eels.

Lord Salisbury, to Joseph Chamberlain, 1899

The diplomat is a person who can tell you to go to hell in such a way that you actually look forward to the trip.

Caskie Stinnet, 1911–98, *Out of the Red*, 1960

A diplomat these days is nothing but a head waiter who's allowed to sit down occasionally.

Peter Ustinov, 1921–2004, *Romanoff and Juliet*, 1956

Diplomacy – lying in state.

Oliver Herford, 1863–1935, American writer and illustrator

Diplomacy is the art of saying, 'Nice doggie!' till you can find a rock.

Wynn Catlin, American writer

There are few ironclad rules of diplomacy but to one there is no exception. When an official reports that talks were useful, it can safely be concluded that nothing was accomplished.

John Kenneth Galbraith, *Foreign Service Journal*, 1969

The chief distinction of a diplomat is that he can say no in such a way that it sounds like yes.

Lester Bowles Pearson, 1897–1972, 14th Prime Minister of Canada, 1963–68, 1972

Diplomacy is the art of letting someone have your way.

Daniele Varè, 1880–1956, Italian diplomat and author

There cannot be a crisis next week. My schedule is already full.

> Henry Kissinger, American diplomat and Nobel Peace Prize recipient, *New York Times Magazine*, 1969

Haig offered me a job explaining US foreign policy to the Chinese – one by one.

> Henry Kissinger, of Alexander Haig, US Army General and Secretary of State under Presidents Nixon and Ford

My advice to any diplomat who wants to have a good press is to have two or three kids and a dog.

> Carl Rowan, 1925–2000, American journalist and author

Diplomacy is to do and say
The nastiest thing in the nicest way.

> Isaac Goldberg, 1887–1938, American author and critic

Ambassador: a politician who is given a job abroad in order to get him out of the country.

> Anon.

Diplomats were invented simply to waste time.

> David Lloyd George, 1863–1945, Liberal Prime Minister, 1916–22, preparing for the Paris Peace Conference, 1918

To say nothing, especially when speaking, is half the art of diplomacy.

> Will Durant, 1885–1981, American writer, historian and philosopher

A diplomat is a man who always remembers a woman's birthday but never remembers her age.

> Robert Frost, 1874–1963, American writer and poet

To jaw-jaw is always better than to war-war.
Winston Churchill, speech at the White House, 1954
Diplomacy is about surviving till the next century – politics
is about surviving till Friday afternoon.
  Antony Jay and Jonathan Lynn, *Yes Prime Minister*, 1986

See also: FOREIGN OFFICE, FOREIGN POLICY

#DOLE, BOB, ATTORNEY AND REPUBLICAN PARTY NOMINEE IN 1996 PRESIDENTIAL ELECTION

We've never had a President named Bob. I think it's about
time we had one.
  Bob Dole

When Bob Dole does smile, he looks as if he's just evicted
a widow.
  Mike Royko, 1932–97, Chicago newspaper columnist

He has never met a tax he hasn't hiked.
  Jack F. Kemp

#DRUGS

Yes, cannabis is dangerous, but no more than other
perfectly legal drugs. It's time for a rethink, and the Tory
party – the funkiest, most jiving party on Earth – is where
it's happening.
  Boris Johnson, Conservative Mayor of London

I think I was once given cocaine but I sneezed so it didn't go up my nose. In fact, it may have been icing sugar.
    Boris Johnson, *Evening Standard*, 2005

E

#ECONOMICS AND ECONOMISTS

If all economists were laid end to end, they would not reach a conclusion.
George Bernard Shaw, 1856–1950, Irish playwright

Anyone who believes in indefinite growth on a finite planet is either mad, or an economist.
David Attenborough, British television presenter

A study of economics usually reveals that the best time to buy anything is last year.
Marty Allen, American stand-up comedian

In all recorded history, there has not been one economist who has had to worry about where his next meal would be coming from.
Peter Drucker, 1909–2005, American writer and 'social ecologist'

One of the greatest pieces of economic wisdom is to know what you don't know.
John Kenneth Galbraith, 1908–2006, Canadian-American economist

Your money does not cause my poverty. Refusal to believe this is at the bottom of most bad economic thinking.

P. J. O'Rourke, *Eat the Rich*, 1998

Economics is an entire scientific discipline of not knowing what you are talking about.

P. J. O'Rourke, *Eat the Rich*, 1998

The only function of economic forecasting is to make astrology look respectable.

Anon.

I learned more about economics from one South Dakota dust storm than I did in all my years in college.

Hubert Humphrey, 1911–78, Democratic Vice President under Lyndon B. Johnson

Give me a one-handed economist! All my economists say, 'On the one hand … on the other'.

Harry S. Truman, 1884–1972, 33rd President of the United States, 1945–53

Everybody is always in favour of general economy and particular expenditure.

Sir Anthony Eden, 1897–1977, Conservative Prime Minister, 1955–57

Economists are people who see something work in practice and wonder if it would work in theory.

Ronald Reagan, 1911–2004, 40th President of the United States, 1981–89

A friend of mine was asked to a costume ball a short time ago. He slapped some egg on his face and went as a liberal economist.

Ronald Reagan

The prestige accorded to math has given economics rigor, but alas, also mortis.

Robert Heilbroner, 1919–2005, American economist and historian

Trickle-down theory – the less than elegant metaphor that if one feeds the horse enough oats, some will pass through to the road for the sparrows.

John Kenneth Galbraith, *The Culture of Contentment*, 1992

Economics is extremely useful as a form of employment for economists.

John Kenneth Galbraith

If you're not confused, you're not paying attention.

Anon., *Wall Street Week*

Trickle-down. The whole theory was this: We have all the money. If we drop some, it's yours. Go for it.

Bill Maher, late-night talk-show host

Balancing the budget is like going to heaven. Everybody wants to do it but nobody wants to do what you have to do to get there.

Phil Gramm, American economist and Democratic congressman, 1979–83

There are three types of economist in the world: those who can count and those who can't.

Eddie George, Governor of the Bank of England, 1993–2003

I especially regret not having been called upon to answer Duncan Weldon's claim that Hayekians are like dentists who have nothing to offer someone who is suffering from a rotten tooth. I might then have been tempted to point out, first of all, that it was pretty cheeky for a British proponent of greater government intervention to be bringing up dentistry.

Professor George Selgin – his preparation for the LSE Keynes versus Hayek debate broadcast on BBC Radio Four, August 2011

Perhaps what appeals to Keynesians about dentistry is that it quite often involves digging holes, and then filling them in.

Brian Micklethwait, comment added to above

[Greek government policy is] known as 'drinking your way back to sobriety'.

Posted on samizdata.net, 2012

See also: BANKS AND BANKING, BIG BUSINESS, BUSINESS, CAPITALISM, CREDIT CRUNCH, ECONOMY, INFLATION, MONEY, POVERTY, RICH AND POOR, STOCK MARKET AND WALL STREET, TAXATION, WEALTH

#ECONOMY, THE

A guy said to me today, 'I assume you're against inflation.'
I said, 'Absolutely – three hundred per cent!'
    Anon.

My friend was facing bankruptcy.
    In his despair, he turned to the Bible for consolation –
and opened it at Chapter 11.
    Anon.

If this isn't a Depression, it's the worst boom in history.
    Anon.

America's national debt totals trillions of dollars. Which
raises the interesting question, how do you repossess a
country?
    Max Kauffman, American vaudeville comedian

A friend of mine told me, 'I'm determined to stay out of
debt – even if I have to borrow money to do so.'
    Sally Poplin, English humorous writer

Some young couples these days are so poor, they're getting
married just for the rice.
    Sally Poplin

About the time we think we can make ends meet, someone
comes along and moves the ends.
    Herbert Hoover, 1874–1964, 31ˢᵗ President of the United
    States, 1929–33

See also: BANKS AND BANKING, BIG BUSINESS, BUSINESS, CAPITALISM, CREDIT CRUNCH, ECONOMICS AND ECONOMISTS, INFLATION, MONEY, POVERTY, RICH AND POOR, STOCK MARKET AND WALL STREET, TAXATION, WEALTH

#EDEN, SIR ANTHONY, 1897–1977, CONSERVATIVE PRIME MINISTER, 1955–57

He is not only a bore but he bores for England.
  Malcolm Muggeridge, 1903–90, English commentator

See also: CONSERVATIVE PARTY

#EDUCATION

Education is an admirable thing, but it is well to remember from time to time that nothing that is worth knowing can be taught.
  Oscar Wilde, 'The Critic as Artist', 1890

The next time some academics tell you how important diversity is, ask how many Republicans there are in their sociology department.
  Thomas Sowell, American economist and political
  philosopher

You know there is a problem with the education system when you realise that, out of the three Rs, only one begins with R.
  Dennis Miller, American comedian and commentator

Education: the path from cocky ignorance to miserable uncertainty.
  Mark Twain, 1835–1910, American writer and humorist

Education is the ability to quote Shakespeare without attributing it to the Bible.
  Anon.

I had a terrible education. I attended a school for emotionally disturbed teachers.
  Woody Allen, American comedian and screenwriter

I never let my schooling interfere with my education.
  Mark Twain

One of my school reports read as follows: 'This boy shows great originality which must be crushed at all costs.'
  Peter Ustinov, 1921–2004, actor and writer

The advantage of a classical education is that it enables you to despise the wealth which it prevents you from achieving.
  Russell Green, American wit

What I have been taught, I have forgotten; what I know, I guessed.
  Charles de Talleyrand, 1754–1838, French diplomat under
  Louis XVI and during the French Revolution

For every person wishing to teach, there are thirty not wanting to be taught.
  Sally Poplin

'Whom are you?' said he, for he had been to night school.
  George Ade, 1866–1944, American humorous writer

Teachers are overworked and underpaid. True, it is an exacting and exhausting business, this damming up the flood of human potentialities.

George B. Leonard, 1923–2010, *Education and Ecstasy*, 1968

An expert is any lecturer from out of town with slides.

Jim Baumgartener, 1943–2011, professor of mathematics

A professor is someone who talks in someone else's sleep.

W. H. Auden, 1907–73, English poet

There is nothing as stupid as an educated man, if you get him off the thing he was educated in.

Will Rogers, 1879–1935, American commentator and humorist

The schoolteacher is certainly underpaid as a child-minder but ludicrously overpaid as an educator.

John Osborne, 1929–94, English playwright

Sam: Education is the silver bullet. Education is everything. We don't need little changes. We need gigantic revolutionary changes. Schools should be palaces. Competition for the best teachers should be fierce. They should be getting six-figure salaries. Schools should be incredibly expensive for government and absolutely free of charge for its citizens, just like national defence. That is my position.

I just haven't figured out how to do it yet.

Aaron Sorkin, *The West Wing*, 2000

#EISENHOWER, DWIGHT D., 1890–1969, 34TH PRESIDENT OF THE UNITED STATES, 1953–61

Eisenhower is the only living Unknown Soldier.
  Robert S. Kerr, 1896–1963, Oklahoma Senator

If I talk over people's heads, Ike must talk under their feet.
  Adlai Stevenson, 1900–1965, Democratic Presidential
  candidate defeated by Eisenhower in 1952 and 1956

This fellow doesn't know any more about politics than a pig knows about Sunday.
  Harry S. Truman

I haven't checked these figures but eighty-seven years ago, I think it was, a number of individuals organised a governmental set-up here in this country, I believe it covered certain eastern areas, with this idea they were following up based on a sort of national-independence arrangement and the program that every individual is just as good as every other individual ...
  Oliver Jensen, *New York Herald Tribune*, 1957

See also: PRESIDENCY, WHITE HOUSE

#ELECTIONS

There is nothing wrong with this country that a good election can't fix.
  Richard Nixon, 1913–94, 37th President of the United States, 1969–74

Do you ever get the feeling that the only reason we have elections is to find out if the polls were right?
    Robert Orben, American jokewriter

At an election meeting an old woman in the crowd called me a bastard. I replied, 'Mother, I told you to stay at home.'
    F. E. Smith, 1st Earl of Birkenhead, 1872–1930, lawyer,
    orator, Conservative statesman

People on whom I do not bother to dote
Are people who do not bother to vote.
    Ogden Nash, 1902–71, 'Election Day is a Holiday', 1933

The people have spoken – the bastards!
    Richard Nixon

The largest turnout at elections is always where there is only one candidate.
    Peter Ustinov

The quickest way to have your family tree traced is to go into politics.
    Bob Hope, 1903–2003, American comedian

British Elections

I was elected by the highly intelligent, far-sighted people of the constituency of Hereford in 1929 – and thrown out by the same besotted mob two years later.
    Frank Owen, 1905–79, British journalist and Liberal
    politician

I keep telling my Tory colleagues: don't have any policies.
A manifesto that has policies alienates people. In 1979 the
manifesto said nothing, which was brilliant.
  Lord Heseltine, Conservative peer and former minister

In elections, when all is said and done, a lot more will be
said than will ever be done.
  Anon.

Election campaigns are like cleaning a window.
The dirt is always on the other side.
  Anon.

American Elections

American youth attributes much more importance to arriving at driver's license age than at voting age.
  Marshall McLuhan, 1911–1980, Canadian educator and
  philosopher

Politics is the gentle art of getting votes from the poor and
campaign funds from the rich by promising to protect each
from the other.
  Oscar Ameringer, 1870–1943, American socialist politician,
  writer and activist

An elected official is one who gets 51 per cent of the
votes cast by 40 per cent of the 60 per cent of voters
who registered.
  Dan Bennett, American comedian

It is not enough to have every intelligent person in the country voting for me – I need a majority.
  Adlai Stevenson

A fool and his money are soon elected.
  Will Rogers

If you want to get elected, shake hands with 25,000 people between now and 7 November.
  Harry S. Truman

During an election campaign, the air is full of speeches and vice versa.
  Henry Adams, 1838–1918, American journalist, novelist and historian

If there had been any formidable body of cannibals in the country, he would have promised to provide them with free missionaries fattened at the taxpayer's expense.
  H. L. Mencken, 1880–1956, *Baltimore Sun*, 1948, of Harry Truman's victory in the 1948 Presidential campaign

Anybody that wants the presidency so much that he'll spend two years organising and campaigning for it is not to be trusted with the office.
  David Broder, 1929–2011, political journalist and pundit, *Washington Post*, 1973

When we got into office, the thing that surprised me most was to find that things were just as bad as we'd been saying they were.

John F. Kennedy, 1917–63, 35th President of the United States, 1961–63, at his birthday party at the White House, 1961

If God wanted us to vote, he would have given us candidates.

Jay Leno, late-night talk-show host

The first thing you do when you want to get elected is to prostitute yourself. You show me a man with courage and conviction and I'll show you a loser.

Ray Kroc, 1902–84, creator of the McDonalds empire

Vote for the man who promises least; he'll be the least disappointing.

Bernard Baruch, 1870–1965, American financier, statesman and philanthropist

Whenever a fellow tells me he's bipartisan, I know he's going to vote against me.

Harry S. Truman

In politics women ... type the letters, lick the stamps, distribute the pamphlets and get out the vote.

Men get elected.

Clare Boothe Luce, 1903–87, American journalist, ambassador and Congresswoman

Ever since the Republican landslide on 8 November it's been getting dark outside a little earlier every day. You notice that?

Mario Cuomo, Democratic Governor of New York 1983–94

2010 US Election

THE REPUBLICAN PARTY:
OUR BRIDGE TO THE 11TH CENTURY.
> Bumper sticker, Bridgeport, Connecticut, 2010

Miss me yet?
> Billboard slogan over picture of George W. Bush,
> Minnesota, 2010

See also: CAMPAIGNING, CANDIDATES, DEBATE,
VOTING

#ENEMIES

Eleanor Roosevelt got even with her enemies in a way that
was almost cruel. She forgave them.
> Ralph McGill, 1898–1969, American journalist and publisher

I make enemies deliberately. They are the *sauce piquante* to
my dish of life.
> Elsa Maxwell, 1883–1963, American gossip columnist and
> hostess

Forgive your enemies, but never forget their names.
> John F. Kennedy

Love your enemy – it'll drive him nuts.
> Anon.

May God have mercy on my enemies, because I won't.
> General George S. Patton, 1885–1945, American soldier
> who served in the First World War and the Second
> World War

You have enemies? Good. That means you've stood up for
something, sometime in your life.
> Winston Churchill, 1874–1965, British orator, politician
> and statesman

A man cannot be too careful in his choice of enemies.
> Oscar Wilde, *The Picture of Dorian Gray*, 1891

Josh: President Bartlet's a good man. He's got a good heart.
He doesn't hold a grudge. That's what he pays me for.
> Aaron Sorkin, *The West Wing*, 'Five Votes Down', 1999

#ENGLAND AND THE ENGLISH

England is perhaps the only great country whose intellectuals are ashamed of their own nationality. In left-wing circles
it is always felt that there is something slightly disgraceful in
being an Englishman and that it is a duty to snigger at every
English institution, from horse racing to suet puddings. It is
a strange fact, but it is unquestionably true that almost any
English intellectual would feel more ashamed of standing to
attention during 'God Save the King' than of stealing from
a poor box.
> George Orwell, 1903–1950, *England Your England*, 1953

The English are a pacifist race – they always hold their wars in someone else's countries.
   Brendan Behan, 1923–64, Irish poet and playwright

No Englishman is ever fairly beaten.
   George Bernard Shaw, *Saint Joan*, 1924

The English never draw a line without blurring it.
   Winston Churchill, speech, House of Commons, 1948

Deploring change is the unchangeable habit of all Englishmen.
   Raymond Postgate, 1896–1971, English journalist, historian and gourmet

An Englishman is a man who lives on an island in the North Sea governed by Scotsmen.
   Philip Guedalla, 1889–1994, *Supers and Supermen*, 1920

The climate of England has been the world's most powerful colonising impulse.
   Russell Green, American wit

Curious race, the English. Once they warm up, there's no telling what they'll do for you.
   S. J. Perelman, 1904–79, *The Rising Gorge*, 1961

An Englishman thinks he is moral when he is only uncomfortable.
   George Bernard Shaw, *Man and Superman*, 1903

England is the most class-ridden country under the sun. It is a land of snobbery and privilege, ruled largely by the old and silly.

George Orwell, 'The Lion and the Unicorn: Socialism and
the English Genius', 1941

But after all, what would the English be without their sweet unreasonableness?

John Galsworthy, 1867–1933, *The Roof*, 1929

The world still consists of two clearly divided groups: the English and the foreigners. One group consists of less than 50 million people; the other of 3,950 million. The latter group does not really count.

George Mikes, 1912–87, *How to Be Decadent*, 1977

The sheer inertia of Englishmen for whom the past was always sacred and inviolable and who prided themselves on their obstinacy. 'We didn't win the war,' thought Sir Godber, 'we just refused to lose it.'

Tom Sharpe, *Porterhouse Blue*, 1974

If you eliminate smoking and gambling, you will be amazed to find that almost all an Englishman's pleasures can be, and mostly are, shared by his dog.

George Bernard Shaw (attrib.)

The English instinctively admire any man who has no talent and is modest about it.

James Agee, 1909–55, American author, poet and
screenwriter

A question. It's addressed to all the equal opportunity, human rights, diet carbon, back room, bleeding heart liberals who advise the government: 'I am English. Why is that a good thing?' I bet they don't have an answer. And until they can come up with one, chances are we'll never win at football again.

Jeremy Clarkson, *Sunday Times*, 2008

See also: BRITAIN AND THE BRITISH

#ENVIRONMENT, THE

I think that I shall never see
A billboard lovely as a tree.
Perhaps, unless the billboards fall,
I'll never see a tree at all.

Ogden Nash, 'Song of the Open Road', 1933

When Ralph Nader tells me he wants my car to be cheap, ugly and slow, he's imposing a way of life on me that I'm going to resist to the bitter end.

Timothy Leary, 1920–96, American psychologist and
writer, of celebrated consumer protection activist (attrib.)

According to a survey in this week's *Time* magazine, 85 per cent of Americans think global warming is happening. The other 15 per cent work for the White House.

Jay Leno

The college idealists who fill the ranks of the environmental movement seem willing to do absolutely anything to save the biosphere, except take science courses and learn something about it.

P. J. O'Rourke, libertarian journalist and commentator

President Bush has a plan [to fight global warming]. He says that if we need to, we can lower the temperature dramatically just by switching from Fahrenheit to Celsius.

Jimmy Kimmel, late-night talk-show host

Man is a complex being; he makes the deserts bloom and lakes die.

Gil Stern, American wit

There are no passengers on Spaceship Earth. Everybody's crew.

Marshall McLuhan

An Inconvenient Truth: There has never been a better time for a movie about global warming set inside an air-conditioned theatre than right now.

Jimmy Kimmel, 2006

Save a Tree. Cancel your liberal newspaper subscription!

T-shirt slogan, Florida 2009

Quite frankly, I can't worry about the earth right now; I'm too worried about the world.

Dennis Miller, American TV comedian, tweet, 2012

Fall is my favourite season in Los Angeles, watching the birds change colour and fall from the trees.

David Letterman, late-night talk-show host

That's the thing about Mother Nature. She really doesn't care what economic bracket you're in.

Whoopi Goldberg, American actor and commentator

Since global warming Eskimos now have twenty different words for water.

John O'Farrell, British journalist, *This Is Your Life*, 2001

Why should I care about future generations? What have they ever done for me?

Groucho Marx, 1890–1977, American comedian and actor

Gordon Brown thinks you can solve climate change by changing your light bulbs. I think you should solve climate change by changing the government.

Siân Berry of the Green Party

Environmentalism, Gaianism, is a religion on the basis of which – illegally under the First Amendment – public policy is being generated. Exhaling carbon dioxide is Original Sin, a reliable source of unlimited power and wealth to a Parasitic Class of politicians, bureaucrats, and cops with which our civilisation now finds itself infested.

L. Neil Smith, libertarian author and political activist

If sunbeams were weapons of war, we would have had solar energy long ago.

George Porter, 1920–2002, British Nobel Prize winning chemist

The earth is like a spaceship that didn't come with an operating manual.
    R. Buckminster Fuller, 1895–1983, American engineer,
    inventor and futurist

IGNORE THE ENVIRONMENT. IT'LL GO AWAY.
    Bumper sticker, Boston, 2005

Remember: a developer is someone who wants to build a
house in the woods. An environmentalist is someone who
already owns a house in the woods.
    Dennis Miller

Underground nuclear testing, defoliation of the rain forests,
toxic waste. Let's put it this way: if the world were a big
apartment, we wouldn't get our deposit back.
    John Ross, actor and comedian

The emotions of the environmentalist lobby are rooted
more in Thoreau than in anger.
    Antony Jay and Jonathan Lynn, *Yes Minister*, 1980

We're told cars are dangerous. It's safer to drive through
South Central Los Angeles than to walk there. We're told
cars are wasteful. Wasteful of what? Oil did a lot of good
sitting in the ground for millions of years. We're told cars
should be replaced with mass transportation. But it's hard
to reach the drive-through window at McDonald's from
a speeding train. And we're told cars cause pollution. A
hundred years ago city streets were ankle deep in horse
excrement. What kind of pollution do you want? Would
you rather die of cancer at eighty or typhoid fever at nine?
    P. J. O'Rourke, *Age and Guile Beat Youth, Innocence, and
    a Bad Haircut*, 1996

The Green Belt is a Labour policy and we intend to build on it.

John Prescott, Labour Deputy Prime Minister

Some good news. Finally, President Bush is going to do something about global warming. He became alarmed when another chunk of ice fell off his mother.

David Letterman

Barbra Streisand told Diane Sawyer that we're in a global warming crisis, and we can expect more and more intense storms, droughts and dust bowls. But before they act, weather experts say they're still waiting to hear from Celine Dion.

Jay Leno, 2005

If we're going to improve the environment, the first thing we should do is duck the government. The second thing we should do is quit being moral. Screw the rights of nature. Nature will have rights as soon as it gets duties. The minute we see birds, trees, bugs, and squirrels picking up litter, giving money to charity, and keeping an eye on our kids at the park, we'll let them vote.

P. J. O'Rourke, *All the Trouble in the World*, 1994

People with a mission to save the earth want the earth to seem worse than it is so their mission will look more important.

P. J. O'Rourke, *All the Trouble in the World*, 1994

So, in the spirit of magnanimity in total crushing victory I would urge readers of this blog not to crow too much about the devastating blow Watts's findings will have on *The Guardian*'s battalion of environment correspondents, on the *New York Times*, on NOAA, on Al Gore, on the Prince of Wales, on the Royal Society, on Professor Muller, or on any of the other rent-seekers, grant-grubbers, eco-loons, crony capitalists, junk scientists, UN apparatchiks, EU technocrats, hideous porcine blobsters, demented squawking parrots, life-free loser trolls, paid CACC-amites and True Believers in the Great Global Warming Religion. That would be plain wrong.

James Delingpole, celebrating a reversal for the warmist cause, 'Global Warming? Yeah right', *Daily Telegraph*, July 2012

See also: OIL

#EQUALITY

The passion for equality produces uniformity which produces mediocrity.

Alexis de Tocqueville, 1805–59, French philosopher and historian

The defect of equality is that we only desire it with our superiors.

Henry Becque, 1837–99, French dramatist

Make all men equal today, and God has so created them that they shall all be unequal tomorrow.

Anthony Trollope, 1815–82, *An Autobiography*, 1883

Not everyone can win and remember, if life was fair, Elvis would still be alive and all the impersonators would be dead.

Johnny Carson, late-night TV host

I wonder how many of the people who profess to believe in the levelling ideas of collectivism and egalitarianism really just believe that they themselves are good for nothing. I mean, how many leftists are animated by a quite reasonable self-loathing? In their hearts they know that they are not going to become scholars or inventors or industrialists or even ordinary good kind people. So they need a way to achieve that smugness for which the left is so justifiably famous. They need a way to achieve self-esteem without merit. Well, there is politics. In an egalitarian world everything will be controlled by politics, and politics requires no merit.

P. J. O'Rourke, speech to the Cato Institute, 1997

Inequality is as dear to the American heart as liberty itself.

W. D. Howells, 1837–1920, *Impressions and Experiences*, 1896

That all men are equal is a proposition to which, in ordinary times, no sane individual has ever given his assent.

Aldous Huxley, 1894–1963, *Proper Studies*, 1927

All animals are equal, but some animals are more equal than others.

George Orwell, *Animal Farm*, 1946

The root of all political evil and human disaster is redistribution of wealth and the drive for 'equality'.

Milo Yiannopoulos, tweet, 2011

Anybody over the age of seven who says that things are not fair needs to have a reality check.

Heather McGregor, businesswoman and columnist, on the public complaining about high pay, BBC Radio Four, 2011

If your only opportunity is to be equal, then it is not opportunity.

Margaret Thatcher, Conservative Prime Minister, 1979–90

I tend to respond of talk about 'social justice' with talk of 'conjugal justice'. Why should only an elite few of the men get the majority of the hot women?

What we need is a program where these men's gorgeous girlfriends or wives should be made to sleep with a corpulent loser or homeless guy periodically so as to promote a more equitable distribution of resources to all individuals and groups.

Posted by YogSothoth, samizdata.net, March 2012

See also: COMMUNISM, FEMINISM, LEFT, LEFT V. RIGHT, MARXISM, SOCIALISM V. CAPITALISM, SOCIALISM

#EUROPE

In my lifetime all our problems have come from mainland Europe and all our solutions have come from the English-speaking nations of the world.

Margaret Thatcher, *The Times*, 1999

Belgium is a country invented by the British to annoy the French.

Charles de Gaulle, 1890–1970, French general and statesman and First President of the Fifth Republic, 1959–69

Belgium is known affectionately to the French as 'the gateway to Germany' and just as affectionately to the Germans
as 'the gateway to France'.
    Tony Hendra, 'EEC! It's the US of E!', *National Lampoon*,
    1976

It seems amazing that no Continental politician is willing to
get to grips with the real crisis facing Europe in the twenty-
first century: the lack of Europeans.
    Mark Steyn, *Daily Telegraph*

Self-righteous Americans? If you want a public culture that
reeks of indestructible faith in its own righteousness, try
Europe – especially when they're talking about America: If
you disagree with Eutopian wisdom, you must be an idiot.
    Mark Steyn, *National Review*

'Europe by the end of this century will be a continent after
the neutron bomb; the grand buildings will still be standing,
but the people who built them will be gone. We are living
through a remarkable period: the self-extinction of the race
who, for good or ill, shaped the modern world.
    Mark Steyn, 2006

Europe's ruling class has effortlessly refined Voltaire: I
disapprove of what you say, and I will defend to the death
my right not to listen to you say it.
    Mark Steyn (attrib.)

*I know that Europe's wonderful, yet something seems
to lack;*
The Past is too much with her, and the people looking back.
  Henry Van Dyke, 1852–1933, American author, educator
  and clergyman

See also: EUROPEAN UNION

#EUROPEAN UNION

UP YOURS DELORS
  Headline in *The Sun*, 1990, reflecting Prime Minister
  Margaret Thatcher's hostility to the policies of Jacques
  Delors, President of the European Commission

Europe is my continent, not my country.
  John Redwood, Conservative Cabinet minister

I can hardly condemn UKIP as a bunch of boss-eyed, foam-
flecked Euro hysterics, when I have been sometimes not far
short of boss-eyed, foam-flecked hysteria myself.
  Boris Johnson, Conservative Mayor of London, on the
  United Kingdom Independence Party

The document is turgid, unreadable, stolid and legalistic. It
has all the intellectual excitement of cold porridge.
  Austin Mitchell, Labour MP, on the European Constitution

I do not see the EEC as a great love affair. It is more like
nine middle-aged couples with failing marriages meeting at
a Brussels hotel for a group grope.
  Kenneth Tynan, 1927–80, English writer and commentator,
  1975

Europe is a place teeming with ill-intentioned persons.
   Margaret Thatcher

Look, I'm actually rather pro-European, actually. I certainly want a European community where one can go and scoff croissants, drink delicious coffee, learn foreign languages and generally make love to foreign women.
   Boris Johnson, quoted in thoughcowardsflinch.com, 2012

See also: EUROPE

F

#FANATICISM

A fanatic is one who won't change his mind and won't change the subject.
  Winston Churchill, 1874–1965, British statesman, orator and writer

The worst vice of the fanatic is his sincerity.
  Oscar Wilde, 1854–1900, Irish playwright

A fanatic is a man who does what he thinks the Lord would do if he knew the facts of the case.
  Finley Peter Dunne, 1867–1936, American humorous writer

Fanaticism consists in redoubling your effort when you have forgotten your aim.
  George Santayana, 1863–1952, *The Life of Reason*, 1905

See also: RADICALISM

#FASCISM

Josh: The number of people whose permission I need before I can do whatever the hell I want... Let me tell you something – there's really a lot to be said for fascism.
  Aaron Sorkin, *The West Wing*, 2001

It is usual to speak of the Fascist objective as the 'beehive state', which does grave injustice to bees. A world of rabbits ruled by stoats would be nearer the mark.
  George Orwell, 1903–50, *The Road to Wigan Pier*, 1937

It will be seen that, as used, the word 'Fascism' is almost entirely meaningless. In conversation, of course, it is used even more wildly than in print. I have heard it applied to farmers, shopkeepers, Social Credit, corporal punishment, fox-hunting, bull-fighting, the 1922 Committee, the 1941 Committee, Kipling, Gandhi, Chiang Kai-Shek, homosexuality, Priestley's broadcasts, Youth Hostels, astrology, women, dogs and I do not know what else.
  ... All one can do for the moment is to use the word with a certain amount of circumspection and not, as is usually done, degrade it to the level of a swearword.
  George Orwell, *What is Fascism*, 1944

A fascist is anyone who disagrees with you.
  John Koski, American wit

See also: CONSERVATIVES AND CONSERVATISM, LEFT V. RIGHT, SOCIALISM

#FEMINISM

A woman without a man is like a fish without a bicycle.
  Gloria Steinem, American journalist, feminist and activist
  (attrib.)

A woman needs a man like a fish needs a net.
Cynthia Heimel, American humorist
Nothing spoils a romance so much as a sense of humour in
the woman.
  Oscar Wilde

Even nowadays a man can't step up and kill a woman without feeling just a bit unchivalrous.
  Robert Benchley, 1889–1945, American humorist

Whatever women do they must do twice as well as men to
be thought half as good. Luckily, this is not difficult.
  Charlotte Whitton, 1896–1975, Mayor of Ottawa,
  Canada, *Canada Month*, 1963

When women are depressed they either eat or go shopping.
Men invade another country.
  Elayne Boosler, American comedian

I'm just a person trapped inside a woman's body.
  Elayne Boosler

Ginger Rogers did everything Fred Astaire did. She just did
it backwards and in high heels.
  Ann Richards, 1933–2006, Democratic Governor of
  Texas, 1991–95, keynote address, Democratic National
  Convention, 1988

A woman has to be twice as good as a man to go half as far.
  Fannie Hurst, 1889–1968, American novelist

God made man and then said, I can do better than that, and
made woman.
  Adela Rogers St Johns, 1894–1988, American journalist,
  novelist and screenwriter

People call me a feminist whenever I express sentiments
that differentiate me from a doormat...
  Rebecca West, 1892–1983, English novelist

If women ran the world we wouldn't have wars, just intense
negotiations every twenty-eight days.
  Robin Williams, American comedian

Of course I'm a feminist. You have to be these days – it's the
only way to pull the chicks.
  Ben Elton, Rick Mayall and Lise Meyer, *The Young Ones*,
  BBC TV, 1988

You say bitch like it's a bad thing!
  T-shirt slogan, Bournemouth, 2009

Don't be sexist. Broads hate that!
  T-shirt slogan, Florida, 1997

Let it all hang out. Let it seem bitchy, catty, dykey, frus-
trated, crazy, nutty, frigid, ridiculous, bitter, embarrassing,
man-hating, libellous, pure, unfair, envious, intuitive, low-
down, stupid, petty, liberating. *We are the women that men
have warned us about.*
  Robin Morgan, 'Goodbye to All That', 1970

I'm furious about the Women's Liberationists. They keep getting up on soapboxes and proclaiming that women are brighter than men. That's true, but it should be kept very quiet or it ruins the whole racket.

Anita Loos, 1888–1981, *The Observer*, 1973

I am working for the time when unqualified blacks, browns and women join the unqualified men in running our government.

Sissy Farenthold, American activist, educator and
Democratic politician, 1974

I think it's about time we voted for senators with breasts. After all, we've been voting for boobs long enough.

Claire Sargent, senatorial candidate, 1992

Nobody can argue any longer about the rights of women. It's like arguing about earthquakes.

Lillian Hellman, 1905–84, American author and playwright (attrib.)

... the women's movement hasn't changed my sex life at all. It wouldn't dare.

Zsa Zsa Gabor, actress, quoted in *Playboy*, 1979

A good part – and definitely the most fun part – of being a feminist, is about frightening men.

Julie Burchill, *Time Out*, 1989

If you were on a sinking ship and yelled, 'Women and children first!' how much feminist opposition do you think you'd get?

... Women want to fight men for equal pay, but how often do they fight a man for the check?

... And any man who questions a woman's physical capabilities gets branded a sexist – but who do they call when there's a spider to be killed?

Convenient feminism – crackpot theory or dangerous lunacy?

Bill Maher, *Politically Incorrect*, 1993

It took women's liberation to make me realise that women can be just as rotten and lousy as men.

Norman Mailer, 1923–2007, *Daily Telegraph*, 1991

Women – the greatest undeveloped natural resource in the world today.

Edward Steichen, 1879–1973, American photographer, painter and museum curator

A woman's work is never done by men.

Sally Poplin, English humorous writer

If it means anything, feminism should be about a woman's right to choose from a list of jobs approved of by other feminists.

Sally Poplin

In the last parliament, the House of Commons had more MPs called John than all the women MPs put together.

Tessa Jowell, Labour MP

I decided to lose weight as I have learned obesity is the leading cause of heart disease, stroke and your flirting at work being construed as harassment.

Pete Johansson, comedian, Edinburgh Festival, 2012

See also: EQUALITY

#FORD, GERALD, 1913-2006, 38TH PRESIDENT OF THE UNITED STATES, 1974-77

A year ago Gerald Ford was unknown throughout America. Now he's unknown throughout the world.
    Norman Mailer, American novelist, 1975

Jerry Ford is so dumb that he can't fart and chew gum at the same time.
    Lyndon B. Johnson, 1908–73, 36th President of the United States, 1963–69

Gerry Ford is a nice guy but he played too much football with his helmet off.
    Lyndon B. Johnson

Richard Nixon impeached himself. He gave us Gerald Ford as his revenge.
    Bella Abzug, 1920–98, American writer and social activist

He's a very nice fellow, but that's not enough, gentlemen. So's my Uncle Fred.
    Hubert Humphrey, 1911–78, Democratic Vice President under Lyndon B. Johnson

Gerald Ford looks like the guy in a science-fiction movie who is first to see the Creature.
    David Frye, 1933–2011, American comedian and impersonator

In the Bob Hope Golf Classic, the participation of President Gerald Ford was more than enough to remind you that the nuclear button was at one stage at the disposal of a man who might have either pressed it by mistake or else pressed it deliberately in order to obtain room service.

> Clive James, Australian poet and critic, *Daily Telegraph*, 2012

See also: PRESIDENCY, WHITE HOUSE

#FOREIGN OFFICE

Progress in the Foreign Service is either vaginal or rectal. You either marry the boss's daughter or you crawl up his bottom.

> Nicholas Monsarrat, 1910–79, British novelist

Tourist in Whitehall to copper. What side is Foreign Office on? That's a good question, sir.

> Andrew Neil, British journalist, tweet, 2012

I'm convinced that there is a small room in the attic of the Foreign Office where future diplomats are taught to stammer.

> Peter Ustinov, 1921–2004, British actor, writer, monologuist

Foreign Office Honours: CMG – 'Call Me God'. KCMG – 'Kindly Call Me God'. GCMG – 'God Calls Me God'.

> Antony Jay and Jonathan Lynn, *Yes Minister*, 1981

See also: DIPLOMACY, FOREIGN POLICY

#FOREIGN POLICY

English policy is to float lazily downstream, occasionally putting out a diplomatic boathook to avoid collisions.
> Lord Salisbury, 1830–1903, Conservative Foreign Secretary
> and three times Prime Minister, letter to Lord Lytton, 1877

Whatever it is that the government does, sensible Americans would prefer that the government do it to somebody else. This is the idea behind foreign policy.
> P. J. O'Rourke, *Parliament of Whores*, 1991

Here is my first principle of foreign policy: good government at home.
> William Ewart Gladstone, 1809–98, four-time Liberal
> Prime Minister

The public aren't interested in foreign affairs. All they want to know is who are the goodies and who are the baddies.
> Antony Jay and Jonathan Lynn, *Yes Minister*, 1986

See also: DIPLOMACY, FOREIGN OFFICE

#FRANCE AND THE FRENCH

The French complain of everything and always.
> Napoleon I, 1769–1821, French revolutionary military and
> political leader

We always have been, we are, and I hope that we always shall be detested in France.
  Duke of Wellington, 1769–1852, British soldier and Prime Minister

How can you govern a nation that has two hundred and forty-six different kinds of cheese?
  Charles de Gaulle, 1890–1970, French general and statesman and First President of the Fifth Republic, 1959–69

The French elections: the Socialists stand accused of staying in Toulon and deserving Toulouse.
  Anon.

Cheese-eatin' surrender monkeys!
  Groundskeeper Willie, *The Simpsons*, 1995

Boy, those French – they have a different word for everything!
  Steve Martin, American comedian

If I were God and were trying to create a nation that would get up the nostrils of Englishmen, I would create the French.
  Julian Barnes, English novelist

In Paris they simply stared when I spoke to them in French; I never did succeed in making those idiots understand their own language.
  Mark Twain, 1835–1910, American writer and humorist

The French approach elections differently than the Americans. They vote.
  Bill Maher, comedian and commentator

France has a new President. He is Socialist François Hollande. He defeated Conservative French President Sarkozy in a Presidential run-off yesterday. Of course, Nicolas Sarkozy handed over power in the traditional French manner. He surrendered.

Jay Leno, late-night talk-show host

France has a new President who lives with a woman that he is not married to. Their relationship is described as French.

Conan O'Brien, late-night talk-show host

French journalists all look as if they've come straight from a highly successful party that began the evening before. British journalists all look as if they got forcibly ejected from the party at 1 a.m. and had to sleep in a skip.

Michael Deacon, *Daily Telegraph*, 2012

#FREE SPEECH

A free society is one where it is safe to be unpopular.

Adlai Stevenson, 1900–1965, Governor of Illinois, Democratic Presidential Candidate 1952 and 1956

Freedom is the freedom to say two plus two makes four. If that is granted, all else follows.

George Orwell

Freedom of opinion can only exist when the government thinks itself secure.

Bertrand Russell, 1872–1970, British philosopher, historian and social critic

And I honor the man who is willing to sink
Half his present repute for the freedom to think,
And, when he has thought, be his cause strong or weak,
Will risk t'other half for the freedom to speak.
   James Russell Lowell, 'A Fable for Critics', 1848

The right to be heard does not automatically include the right to be taken seriously.
   Hubert H. Humphrey, speech reported in the *New York Times*, 1965

You know what's wrong with this country? Everyone gets the chance to have their fair say.
   Bill Clinton, 42nd President of the United States, 1993–2001

If we don't believe in freedom of expression for people we despise, we don't believe in it at all.
   Noam Chomsky, philosopher

Freedom isn't for wimps.
   Neal Boortz, American radio host and political commentator

See also: DEBATE, LIBERTY

G

#GERMANY AND THE GERMANS

Whenever the literary German dives into a sentence, that is
the last you are going to see of him till he emerges on the
other side of his Atlantic with his verb in his mouth.
  Mark Twain, 1835–1910, *A Connecticut Yankee in King
  Arthur's Court*, 1889

Because of their cuisine, Germans don't consider farting
rude. They'd certainly be out of luck if they did.
  P. J. O'Rourke, *Modern Manners*, 1989

I married a German. Every night I dress up as Poland and
he invades me.
  Bette Midler, American entertainer

The reason there is so little crime in Germany is that it's
against the law.
  Alex Levin, American wit

You can always reason with a German. You can always
reason with a barnyard animal, too, for all the good it does.
  P. J. O'Rourke, *Holidays in Hell*, 1989

#GLADSTONE, WILLIAM EWART, 1809–98, LIBERAL PRIME MINISTER, 1868–74, 1880–85, 1886, 1892–94

A misfortune is if Gladstone fell into the Thames; a calamity would be if someone pulled him out.
   Benjamin Disraeli, 1804–81, writer and Conservative
   Prime Minister, 1874–80

It is said that Mr Gladstone could persuade most people of most things and himself of anything.
   W. R. Inge, 1860–1954, Dean of St Paul's Cathedral

I saw Mr Gladstone in the street last night. I waited and waited but no cab ran him over.
   Eliza Savage, Victorian floozie

I don't object to Gladstone always having the ace of trumps up his sleeve, but merely to his belief that God Almighty put it there.
   Henry Labouchere, 1831–1912, prominent Whig and
   Liberal Party politician

Mr Gladstone speaks to me as if I were a public meeting.
   Queen Victoria, 1819–1901 (attrib.)

They told me how Mr Gladstone read Homer for fun, which I thought served him right.
   Winston Churchill, 1874–1965, British statesman, orator
   and writer, *My Early Life*, 1930

He has not a single redeeming defect.
   Benjamin Disraeli (attrib.)

... honest in the most odious sense of the word.
  Benjamin Disraeli (attrib.)

See also: LIBERALS AND LIBERALISM

#GOVERNMENT

The art of government consists of taking as much money as
possible from one class of citizens to give to the other.
  Voltaire, 1694–1778, French writer, historian and
  philosopher

Were we directed from Washington when to sow, and when
to reap, we should soon want bread.
  Thomas Jefferson, 1743–1826, *Memoirs of Thomas
  Jefferson*, 1821

The best government is a benevolent tyranny tempered by
an occasional assassination.
  Voltaire

The office of government is not to confer happiness but
to give men the opportunity to work out happiness for
themselves.
  William Ellery Channing, American Unitarian preacher in
  the early nineteenth century

Every time I fill a vacant office I make ten malcontents and
one ingrate.
  Louis XIV, quoted by Molière

The best government is that which governs least.
John L. O'Sullivan, *United States Magazine and Democratic Review*, 1837

That fatal drollery called a representative government.
Benjamin Disraeli, *Tancred*, 1847

Working for a federal agency was like trying to dislodge a prune skin from the roof of the mouth. More enterprise went into the job than could be justified by the result.
Caskie Stinnet, 1911–98, American editor and writer

The government solution to any problem is usually at least as bad as the problem.
Milton Friedman, 1912–2006, American economist

Nothing is so permanent as a temporary government program.
Milton Friedman

I learned in business that you had to be very careful when you told somebody that's working for you to do something, because the chances were very high he'd do it. In government, you don't have to worry about that.
George Shultz, American economist, statesman and businessman

As far as I am concerned, dirty tricks are part and parcel of effective government.
Alan Clark, 1928–99, Conservative MP and diarist, quoted in the *Sunday Times*, 1993

At the very heart of British government there is a luxuriant and voluntary exclusion of talent.
> Brian Chapman, British academic

My faith in the people governing is, on the whole, infinitesimal; my faith in the people governed is, on the whole, illimitable.
> Charles Dickens, 1812–70, English novelist and social
> critic, speech, Birmingham, 1869

The state is like the human body. Not all of its functions are dignified.
> Anatole France, 1844–1924, *Les Opinions de M. Jerome
> Coignard*, 1893

A career in politics is no preparation for government.
> Antony Jay and Jonathan Lynn, *Yes Minister*, 1980

If government were a product, selling it would be illegal.
> P. J. O'Rourke, *The Liberty Manifesto*, 1993

If the answer is more politicians, you are asking the wrong question.
> John Major, Conservative Prime Minister, 1990–1997
> (attrib.)

The ideal government minister may well be someone who has no itch to run other people's lives.
> Edward Grey, 1862–1933, British Foreign Secretary from
> 1905 to 1916

Every government will do as much harm as it can and as much good as it must.
> Willmott Lewis, 1877–1950, British journalist

The single most exciting thing you encounter in government is competence, because it's so rare.
Daniel Patrick Moynihan, 1927–2003, Democratic Senator

A friend of mine said, 'I don't know why they're picking on the regulators.
'They haven't done anything!'
Sally Poplin, English humorous writer

Government is like a big baby – an alimentary canal with a big appetite at one end and no responsibility at the other.
Ronald Reagan, 1911–2004, 40th President of the United States, 1981–89, in 1966

One of the greatest delusions of the world is the hope that the evils in this world are to be cured by legislation.
Thomas B. Reed, 1839–1902, speaker of the House of Representatives, 1889–91, 1895–99

To borrow a quotation from John F. Kennedy: 'Ask not what your country can do for you ...'
'But how much it's going to cost you for them to do it.'
Anon.

The most terrifying words in the English language are, 'I'm from the government and I'm here to help.'
Ronald Reagan, 1966

Giving money and power to government is like giving whiskey and car keys to teenage boys.
P. J. O'Rourke, *Parliament of Whores*, 1991

The supply of government exceeds the demand.
  Lewis H. Lapham, American essayist and editor

We must not look to government to solve our problems.
Government is the problem.
  Ronald Reagan, 1966

We must remember that for every instance of the government's demonstrating the intelligence of a yam, there is also
an instance of the government's rising to the level of a far
more complex vegetable, such as the turnip.
  Dave Barry, 'Invasion of the Money Snatchers', 1994

I don't make jokes. I just watch the government and report
the facts.
  Will Rogers, 1879–1935, American commentator and
  humorist

Government is too big and important to be left to the
politicians.
  Chester Bowles, 1901–86, American diplomat and
  Democratic politician

Let each of us ask, not just what government can do for me
but what can I do for myself?
  Richard Nixon, 1913–94, 37th President of the United
  States, 1969–74, in a rebuttal of JFK's inaugural, 'Ask not
  what your country can do for you. Ask what you can do
  for your country.'

My brother Bob doesn't want to be in government. He
promised Dad he'd go straight.
  John F. Kennedy, 1917–63, 35th President of the United
  States, 1961–63

The great problem in government is that it never goes bankrupt.
>   Jerry Brown, Democratic politician and 34th Governor of
>   California

Be thankful that we're not getting all the government we're paying for.
>   Will Rogers

The worst thing in the world, next to anarchy, is government.
>   Henry Ward Beecher, 1813–87, *Proverbs from Plymouth
>   Pulpit*, 1887

DON'T WANT GOVERNMENT?
MOVE TO SOMALIA!
>   Bumper sticker, New York, 2011

Ineptocracy – A new word for our times
A system of government where the least capable to lead are elected by the least capable of producing, and where the members of society least likely to sustain themselves or succeed, are rewarded with goods and services paid for by the confiscated wealth of a diminishing number of producers.
>   Ukipwebmaster, March 2012

See also: BUREAUCRACY, CIVIL SERVICE
AND WHITEHALL, LOCAL GOVERNMENT,
WASHINGTON

H

#HARDING, WARREN G., 1865-1923, 29TH PRESIDENT OF THE UNITED STATES, 1921-23

He writes the worst English that I have ever encountered. It reminds me of a string of wet sponges; it reminds me of tattered washing on the line; it reminds me of stale bean soup, of college yells, of dogs barking idiotically through endless nights. It is so bad that a sort of grandeur creeps into it. It drags itself out of the dark abysm of pish, and crawls insanely up to the topmost pinnacle of posh. It is rumble and bumble. It is flap and doodle. It is balder and dash.

H. L. Mencken, 1880–1956, on Warren G. Harding, *Baltimore Evening Sun*, 1921

His speeches left the impression of an army of pompous phrases moving over the landscape in search of an idea; sometimes these meandering words would actually capture a straggling thought and bear it triumphantly a prisoner in their midst, until it died of servitude and overwork.

William G. McAdoo, 1863–1941, lawyer, senator and unsuccessful contender for Democratic nomination for President, 1920 and 1924

... a tin-horn politician with the manner of a rural corn doctor and the mien of a ham actor.

H. L. Mencken

#HEALTH

There's another advantage to being poor. A doctor will cure you faster.

Kin Hubbard, 1868–1930, American cartoonist, humorist and journalist

God heals and the doctor takes the fee.

Benjamin Franklin, 1706–90, American statesman and Founding Father

A hospital bed is a parked taxi with the meter running.

Groucho Marx, 1890–1977, American comedian and actor

I have been thinking about the healthcare problem and how to pay for healthcare. If you took all the money the Republicans have spent trying to stop healthcare and all the money Democrats have spent trying to get healthcare, we could afford healthcare.

Jay Leno, late-night talk-show host, 2011

Congressman John Boehner told a crowd of protesters yesterday that the new healthcare bill was the 'greatest threat to freedom [he's] ever seen'. And then the Taliban was like, 'Uh, helloooo? What?!'

Jimmy Fallon, late-night talk-show host, 2010

The big news was the Senate yesterday – the finance committee – rejected the Democrats' healthcare plan, the one with the public option. Meanwhile, the Republicans are offering their own healthcare plan. It's called, 'Stop Crying and Take an Advil'.
Jimmy Fallon

Healthy citizens are the greatest asset any country can have.
Winston Churchill, 1874–1965, British statesman, orator and writer

The Republicans, whose healthcare plan consists of, 'Just Say No to Sickness'.
Kevin Pollack, American actor and comedian

'Eating and Drinking Can Kill', says Government
A new official study has shown a startling correlation between the consumption of all forms of food and drink and the incidence of fatality in the population of the UK as a whole.

The study's remarkable finding is that almost all of the people who died in Britain last year did so after consuming food, drink or both.

... Said the Chief Medical Officer last night, 'We are hoping to make a start on tackling this national crisis by putting health warnings on all food and drink products and making it illegal to eat or drink inside public buildings such as pubs, restaurants and cafes.'
Private Eye, 2012

#HEATH, EDWARD, 1916–2005, CONSERVATIVE PRIME MINISTER, 1970–74

He resented the success of Margaret Thatcher for the last thirty years of his life. It ate away at him, turning him into a squat stewpot of boiling hatred... There was so much bile in him that it was only a surprise that it did not ooze out of the wet corners of his sparsely lashed eyes.
 Quentin Letts, *50 People Who Buggered up Britain*, 2008

... a shiver waiting for a spine to run up.
 Harold Wilson, 1916–95, Labour Prime Minister, 1964–70,
 1974–76

Receiving support from Ted Heath in a by-election is like being measured by an undertaker.
 George Gardiner, 1935–2002, Conservative politician and
 journalist

Mr Heath envies me two things. First, I have a first-class honours degree. Second, I am a gentleman.
 Quintin Hogg, 1907–2001, Conservative peer

If politicians lived on praise and thanks, they'd be forced into some other line of business.
 Edward Heath

I have no interest in sailing around the world. Not that there is any lack of requests for me to do so.
 Edward Heath

#HOMOSEXUALITY

What do you call a man who marries another man?
A vicar!
    Benny Hill, 1924–92, British comedian

Why is it that, as a culture, we are more comfortable seeing
two men holding guns than holding hands?
    Ernest Gaines, African-American novelist

My own belief is that there is hardly anyone whose sexual
life, if it were broadcast, would not fill the world at large
with surprise and horror.
    W. Somerset Maugham, 1874–1965, British playwright and
    novelist

It always seemed to me a bit pointless to disapprove of
homosexuality. It's like disapproving of rain.
    Francis Maude, Conservative politician

Here is a little tip for all of you: don't come out to your
father in a moving vehicle.
    Kate Clinton, American writer and comedian

I'd rather be black than gay because when you're black you
don't have to tell your mother.
    Charles Pierce, 1926–99, American female impersonator,
    1980

I'm in favour of gay marriage. Then, at least both people
are excited about planning the wedding.
    Jay Leno

I'm against gay marriage. I think marriage is a sacred union between a man and a pregnant woman.
    Craig Kilborn, late-night talk-show host

My Aunt Lorraine said, 'Bob, you're gay. Are you seeing a psychiatrist?' I said, 'No, I'm seeing a lieutenant in the Navy.'
    Bob Smith, American comedian

On Wednesday, Maine became the fifth state to legalise gay marriage, after Governor Balducci signed a same-sex marriage bill into law. It's the best news for gays in Maine since L. L. Bean introduced a line of assless duck-waders.
    Seth Meyers, *Saturday Night Live*, 2009

First Lady Michelle Obama appears on *Sesame Street* to celebrate the show's fortieth anniversary. It's going to be a big episode. Yes, sources say the episode gets a little tense when Ernie and Bert ask the First Lady why her husband's dragging his feet on gay marriage.
    Conan O'Brien, late-night talk-show host, 2009

When you're a gay couple getting married, who gets the bachelor party? Who goes downstairs in the middle of the night to check on the noise? Who forgets the anniversary? Who refuses to stop and ask for directions? And which one of you will take forever to get ready?
    David Letterman, late-night talk-show host, 2012

Gays are now allowed to serve openly in the military. So maybe our next war could be a musical.
    David Letterman

#HOOVER, HERBERT, 1874-1964, 31ST PRESIDENT OF THE UNITED STATES, 1929-33

That man has offered me unsolicited advice for six years, all of it bad.

> Calvin Coolidge, 1872–1933, 30th President of the United States, 1923–29

In 1932, lame duck President Herbert Hoover was so desperate to remain in the White House that he dressed up as Eleanor Roosevelt. When FDR discovered the hoax in 1936, the two men decided to stay together for the sake of the children.

> Johnny Carson, 1925–2005, late-night TV host

I'm the only person of distinction who's ever had a depression named for him.

> Herbert Hoover

I was just standing out in front watching the other acts when a lady walked up to me in the lobby and said, 'Pardon me, young man, could you tell me where I could find the rest room?' and I said, 'It's just around the corner.' 'Don't give me that Hoover talk,' she said. 'I'm serious.'

> Al Boasberg, 1903–2003, American comedian, 'For Bob Hope', 1930

See also: PRESIDENCY, WHITE HOUSE

#HOUSE OF COMMONS

No man is a regular in his attendance in the House of Commons until he is married.

Benjamin Disraeli, 1804–81, writer and Conservative
Prime Minister, 1874–80

When in that House MPs divide,
If they've a brain and cerebellum, too,
They've got to leave that brain outside,
And vote just as their leaders tell 'em to.
But then the prospect of a lot
Of dull MPs in close proximity,
All thinking for themselves, is what
No man can face with equanimity.

W. S. Gilbert, *Iolanthe*, 1882

Only people who look dull ever get into the House of Commons, and only people who are dull ever succeed there.

Oscar Wilde, *An Ideal Husband*, 1895

The last person who went into the House of Commons with good intentions was Guy Fawkes.

Alfred Wintle, 1897–1966, British military officer in the
First and Second World Wars

The Speaker's eye: the most elusive organ that Nature ever created.

Stanley Baldwin, 1867–1947, Conservative politician and
three-time Prime Minister

I do not know what the Right Hon. Lady the Minister for
Education [Miss Florence Horsbrugh] is grinning at. I was
told by one of my Hon. friends this afternoon that this is a
face which has sunk a thousand scholarships.
    Aneurin Bevan, Labour politician, speech on cuts in the
    education budget, House Of Commons, 1953

If, from any speech in the House, one begins to see any
results within five to ten years after it has been delivered,
one will have done very well indeed.
    Robert (later Lord) Boothby, 1900–1986, Conservative
    MP, 1936

... a Bill to make attendance at the House of Commons
compulsory has been passed by three votes to two.
    David Frost and Antony Jay, *To England with Love*, 1967

I count my blessings for the fact I don't have to go into
that pit that John Major stands in, nose-to-nose with the
opposition, all yelling at each other.
    George H. W. Bush, 41st President of the United States,
    1989–93, speech at the 1991 Republican National
    Convention

This afternoon I slept for two hours in the library of the
House of Commons. A deep House of Commons sleep –
rich, deep and guilty.
    Henry Channon, 1897–1958, Conservative MP, author
    and diarist

... the longest-running farce in the West End.
    Cyril Smith, Liberal MP, *Big Cyril*, 1977

In the House of Commons, sword-fighting is strictly taboo. Back-stabbing, on the other hand, is quite a different matter.

Gyles Brandreth, British writer, broadcaster and former Conservative MP

There is no place where a man can occupy himself more intensively or usefully, and no place where he can hold down his job by doing so little.

Nigel Nicolson, British Conservative politician and author, on the House of Commons, *People and Parliament*, 1958

... much of what happens in the Commons is a performance of pantomime artifice: the cheers, the jeers, the heckles. I particularly enjoy the eruptions of fake laughter from backbenchers whenever their leader cracks a joke. You know it's fake because they slap their thighs, just like absolutely no one in the real world does.

Michael Deacon, *Daily Telegraph*, 2011

But then Ms Harman sprang a little surprise. Someone had written her a joke. On the rare occasions Ms Harman finds a joke incorporated into her script, she approaches the challenge gamely but with obvious trepidation, like a middle-aged Sunday School teacher who has been asked to ride a unicycle for charity.

Michael Deacon, *Daily Telegraph*, 2012, on a speech by Harriet Harman

See also: HOUSE OF LORDS, PARLIAMENT

#HOUSE OF LORDS

A severe though not unfriendly critic of our institutions said that the cure for admiring the House of Lords was to go and look at it.
Walter Bagehot, 1826–77, *The English Constitution*, 1867

... a body of 500 men chosen at random from amongst the unemployed.
David Lloyd George, 1863–1945, Liberal Prime Minister, 1916–22

The House of Lords is like a glass of champagne that has stood for five days.
Clement Attlee, 1883–1967, Labour Prime Minister, 1945–51

It is, I think, good evidence of life after death.
Lord Soper, 1903–98, Methodist minister and socialist, *The Listener,* 1978

The House of Lords must be the only institution in the world which is kept efficient by the persistent absenteeism of most of its members,
Herbert Samuel, 1870–1963, British politician and diplomat, *News Review*, 1948

It was but a few weeks since he had taken his seat in the House of Lords and, this afternoon, for want of anything better to do, he strayed in and sat in it.
Max Beerbohm, 1872–1956, English essayist, parodist and novelist

The other night I dreamed that I was addressing the House of Lords. Then I woke up and by God I was.
    Duke of Devonshire, 1833–1908, Conservative politician

I oppose the plan to reform the House of Lords. I will be sad, if I look down after my death and don't see my son asleep on the same benches on which I slept.
    Lord Onslow, 1938–2011, Conservative hereditary peer

Like many other anachronisms in British public life, the House of Lords has one supreme merit. It works.
    Lord Boothby, Conservative peer (attrib.)

The House of Lords is a perfect eventide home.
    Lady Stocks, 1891–1975, British writer and broadcaster,
    1970

The House of Lords is a model of how to care for the elderly.
    Frank Field, Labour MP, 1981

Going from the Commons to the Lords is like being moved from the animals to the vegetables.
    Antony Jay and Jonathan Lynn, *Yes Minister*, 1981

... on great matters of State it does have the vital constitutional right to say 'Yes' or 'Yes, but not for a few weeks.'
    David Frost and Antony Jay, *To England with Love*, 1967

A statesman is a dead politician. I'm in the home of the living dead – the House of Lords.
    Denis Healey, Labour Chancellor of the Exchequer,
    1974–79

The House of Lords is the British Upper Mongolia for
retired politicians.

    Tony Benn, Labour politician, quoted in *The Observer*,
    1962

See also: HOUSE OF COMMONS, PARLIAMENT

I

#IMMIGRATION

Immigration is the sincerest form of flattery.
  Jack Paar, 1918–2004, American entertainer

Not only does Europe consent to its demographic disap-
pearance, but it interprets it as proof of its moral superiority.
  Daily Telegraph blog commenter, 2011

My folks didn't come over on the *Mayflower*, but they were
there to meet the boat.
  Will Rogers, 1879–1935, American commentator and
  humorist

GIVE ME YOUR TIRED, YOUR POOR, YOUR HUDDLED MASSES
YEARNING TO BREAK FREE.
THIS OFFER NOT VALID IN ARIZONA.
  Pro-immigration protest sign, Arizona, 2011

We all know there is a long tradition of great nations
importing foreign workers to do their farm work. After all,
it was the ancient Israelites who built the first food pyra-
mids... But this is America. I don't want a tomato picked by
a Mexican. I want it picked by an American. Then sliced by

a Guatemalan, and served by a Venezuelan in a spa where a Chilean gives me a Brazilian.

My great-grandfather did not travel across 4,000 miles of the Atlantic Ocean to see this country overrun by immigrants.

Stephen Colbert, American comedian, testifying before
Congress on behalf of the United Farm Workers Union, 2010

On entering the United States I was given a form to fill in by the Immigration Authority. To the question, 'Is it your intention to overthrow the government of the US by force?' I gave the written answer, 'Sole purpose of visit'.

Gilbert Harding, 1907–60, English broadcaster

All the problems we face in the United States today can be traced to an unenlightened immigration policy on the part of the American Indian.

Pat Paulsen, 1927–97, American comedian and satirist

Remember always that all of us are descended from immigrants.

Franklin D. Roosevelt, 1882–1945, 32nd President of the
United States, 1933–45

I'm in favour of liberalised immigration because of the effect it would have on restaurants. I'd let just about everybody in except the English.

Calvin Trillin, American wit

The economy is still hurting. Thirty per cent of Americans are so disillusioned, they are thinking of moving back to Mexico.

Jay Leno, late-night talk-show host, 2011

Alabama just passed a tough immigration law that requires schools to find out if students are in the country illegally. Fortunately, schools know what to look for when identifying foreign students: high test scores.

Jimmy Fallon, late-night talk-show host, 2012

As you know, Arizona recently passed the toughest anti-immigration bill in American history. The idea behind this bill is to drive illegal immigrants out of Arizona and back to their homeland of Los Angeles.

Jay Leno

Arizona has passed the strictest immigration bill in American history. A hundred people have been stopped already – and that was just in one van.

Jay Leno

Arizona's Governor had been stalling, you know, on signing this. She said it did not reflect any ambivalence about the bill. She just wanted to make sure her pool was clean and her lawn was mowed before she signed.

Bill Maher, late-night talk-show host

They say there are about 12 million illegal immigrants in this country. But if you ask a native American, that number is more like 300 million.

David Letterman, late-night talk-show host

President Bush also said in his speech that immigrants have to learn English. The immigrants said, 'Hey, you first.'

Jay Leno

#IMPERIALISM

Americans think of themselves as a huge rescue squad on 24-hour call to any spot on the globe where dispute and conflict may erupt.
  Eldridge Cleaver, 1935–98, black activist

No colonisation without misrepresentation.
  Simeon Strunsky, 1879–1948, Jewish-American essayist

We should keep [the Panama Canal]. After all, we stole it fair and square.
  S. I. Hayakawa, 1906–92, American academic and
  politician

We don't know what we want but we are ready to bite somebody to get it.
  Will Rogers

#INFLATION

Among the things that money can't buy is what it used to.
  Max Kauffman, American comedian

Time for belt tightening. You can't live on a million a year anymore.
  Randy Newman, American songwriter, 1983

There was a time when a fool and his money were soon parted, but now it happens to everyone.
  Adlai Stevenson, 1900–1965, Governor of Illinois,
  Democratic Presidential Candidate 1952 and 1956

Americans are getting stronger. Twenty years ago, it took two people to carry ten dollars' worth of groceries. Today, a five-year-old can do it.

> Henny Youngman, 1908–98, American comedian

See also: BANKS AND BANKING, BIG BUSINESS, BUSINESS, CAPITALISM, CREDIT CRUNCH, ECONOMICS AND ECONOMISTS, ECONOMY, MONEY, POVERTY, RICH AND POOR, STOCK MARKET AND WALL STREET, TAXATION, WEALTH

#INSULTS

I've been called worse things by better men.

> Pierre Elliott Trudeau, 1919–2000, 15th Prime Minister of Canada, 1968–79, 1980–84, after Richard Nixon had called him an 'asshole'

Nineteenth-Century Insults

The Right Honourable Gentleman is reminiscent of a poker. The only difference is that a poker gives off the occasional signs of warmth.

> Benjamin Disraeli, 1804–81, writer and Conservative Prime Minister, 1874–80, of previous Conservative Prime Minister Sir Robert Peel

When he rises to speak, he does not know what he is going to say. When he is speaking, he does not know what he is saying and, when he sits down, he does not know what he has said.

> William Ewart Gladstone, 1809–98, four-time Liberal Prime Minister, of Lord Derby, Conservative Prime Minister

If a traveller were informed that such a man was Leader of the House of Commons, he might begin to comprehend how the Egyptians worshipped an insect.

　　Benjamin Disraeli, of Lord John Russell, English Whig and
　　Liberal politician and Prime Minister

I met Curzon in Downing Street, from whom I got the sort of greeting a corpse would give an undertaker.

　　Stanley Baldwin, 1867–1947, Conservative politician
　　and three-time Prime Minister, of Lord Curzon, fellow
　　Conservative

Dangerous as an enemy, untrustworthy as a friend, but fatal as a colleague.

　　Sir Hercules Robinson, 1824–97, colonial governor, of
　　politician and statesman Joseph Chamberlain

James Garfield has shown that he is not possessed of the backbone of an angleworm.

　　Ulysses S. Grant, 1822–85, Civil War commander and 18th
　　President of the United States, of the 20th President of the
　　United States

His argument is as thin as the homoeopathic soup that was made by boiling the shadow of a pigeon that had been starved to death.

　　Abraham Lincoln, 1809–65, 16th President of the United
　　States, 1861–65, of Stephen A. Douglas, his Democratic
　　opponent in the 1860 Presidential election

He looked at me as if I was a side dish he hadn't ordered.
    Ring Lardner, 1915–2000, American humorous writer, of
    William Taft, 27th President of the United States

I have never found, in a long experience of politics, that
criticism is ever inhibited by ignorance.
    Harold Macmillan, 1894–1986, Conservative Prime
    Minister, 1957–63, aimed at his son Maurice who had writ-
    ten a letter to *The Times* criticising the government, 1963

He who throws mud loses ground.
    Adlai Stevenson

It is not necessary that every time he rises he should give his
famous imitation of a semi-house-trained polecat.
    Michael Foot, 1913–2010, Labour politician, of Conservative
    Norman Tebbit, House of Commons, 1978

Lord Derby is a very weak-minded fellow, I'm afraid, and,
like the feather pillow, bears the marks of the last person
who has sat on him.
    Earl Douglas Haig, 1861–1928, senior British army officer
    during the First World War, of Lord Derby, Conservative
    politician and Secretary of State for War

When they circumcised Herbert Samuel, they threw away
the wrong bit.
    David Lloyd George, 1863–1945, Liberal Prime Minister,
    1916–22, of Herbert Samuel, politician and diplomat

He has sat on the fence for so long, the iron has entered
into his soul.
    David Lloyd George

George Bush is living proof that having a dream and a goal and burning desire to work hard to realise them ... doesn't always work.

    Anon.

Yes, you can always rely on George Bush to do the right thing too late and the wrong thing too soon.

    Anon.

Why won't John McCain tell us the truth about this?
Is it too much to ask of a candidate that he be candid?

    Anon., of Republican Presidential nominee John McCain
    in 2008 US election

It would be wrong to suggest that Neil Hamilton is his own worst enemy, when there are so many others better qualified for the post.

    Craig Brown, English satirist, of Conservative MP Neil
    Hamilton

Robin Cook's misfortune is to sound as if his voice never broke – but his behaviour encourages this view.

    Jacob Rees-Mogg, Conservative MP

William McKinley has no more backbone than a chocolate éclair.

    Theodore Roosevelt, 1858–1919, 26th President of the
    United States, 1901–09, of the 25th President of the United
    States

They couldn't pour piss out of a shoe if the instructions were written on the heel.

    Lyndon B. Johnson, 1908–73, 36th President of the United
    States, 1963–69

Dan Quayle is more stupid than Ronald Reagan put together.
   Matt Groening, writer and cartoonist, of the US Vice
   President under George H. W. Bush

Lew asked me a little earlier if Tom [DeLay] ever smiled. I
said, 'I don't know, I've only known him nine years.'
   George W. Bush, speech, Washington 2002

It's certainly possible to keep a good bottle just a bit too long.
   Liam Fox, Conservative minister, on Labour's Dennis
   Skinner, House of Commons, October 2011

There but for the grace of God, goes God.
   Winston Churchill, 1874–1965, British statesman, orator
   and writer, of Labour minister Stafford Cripps

If you have half a mind to read their manifesto, that's probably all you'll need.
   Anon.

If he had been given an enema, he could have been buried
in a matchbox.
   Christopher Hitchens, 1949–2011, British-American journalist and controversialist, on televangelist and conservative commentator Jerry Falwell

She's upstairs filing her teeth.
   Groucho Marx, 1890–1977, American comedian and actor,
   of Eleanor Roosevelt, social activist and wife of President
   Franklin D. Roosevelt

Walter Mondale has all the charisma of a speed bump.
   Will Durst, comedian, of the Democratic Vice President

That part of his speech was rather like being savaged by a
dead sheep.
     Denis Healey, Labour Chancellor of the Exchequer, 1974–
     79, on a speech in the House of Commons by Geoffrey
     Howe, 1978

My opponent has a problem. He won't get elected unless things
get worse – and things won't get worse unless he's elected.
     George W. Bush, 43rd President of the United States,
     2002–09

Sir Stafford Cripps has a brilliant mind until he makes it up.
     Margot Asquith, 1864–1945, Anglo-Scottish socialite and
     wit, of the British Labour politician

When Al Gore gives a fireside chat, the fire goes out.
     Bob Dole, American attorney and Republican politician, of
     Democratic US Vice President

... like having a wardrobe fall on top of you with the key
sticking out.
     Anonymous woman, describing sex with portly
     Conservative MP, Nicholas Soames

He's calling me the political equivalent of the house wine at
a suburban Indian restaurant.
     Armando Iannucci, *The Thick Of It*, BBC TV, 2005

All these hands all over the place! You were like a sweaty
octopus trying to unhook a bra.
     Armando Iannucci, *The Thick Of It*, BBC TV, 2005,
     describing a TV interview

Waking up to find self on the Nadine Dorries naughty step. Which is a pity as I spend my entire time worrying about what she thinks. (ahem).

Louise Mensch, former MP, of fellow Conservative who had criticised her, tweet, August 2012

Senator, I served with Jack Kennedy, I knew Jack Kennedy, Jack Kennedy was a friend of mine. Senator, you're no Jack Kennedy.

Senator Lloyd Bentsen to Dan Quayle, during 1988 Vice-Presidential debate, during which Senator Quayle seemed to frequently compare himself to John Kennedy.

#INTERNET, THE

Bill Gates is a very rich man today ... and do you want to know why? The answer is one word: versions.

Dave Barry, *Miami Herald*

Give a man a fish and you feed him for a day. Teach him to use the net and he won't bother you for weeks.

Anon.

The internet is the most important single development in the history of human communication since the invention of call waiting.

Dave Barry, *Miami Herald*

NEVER go past the forty-third page of a Google search result. No one has ever been that far and you MAY fall off the edge of the internet.

ArenaFlowers, tweet, 2012

Not gonna lie. Before Google, I used to constantly Encyclopedia Britannica myself.

Sid Karger, tweet, 2012

Let me Bing search that. Said no one ever.
  Someecards, July 2012

I love to watch fights on the internet. There's nothing funnier than watching two adults suddenly go CAPS LOCK ON EACH OTHER.
  Someecards, July 2012

Hugh: How long since you've had sex?
Glenn: That is between me and my internet service provider.
  Armando Iannucci, *The Thick Of It*, BBC TV, 2005

See also: SOCIAL MEDIA

#IRAQ WAR

Q: What are they calling the Germans, French and Belgians, at the Pentagon?
A: 'The Axis of Weasels.'
  Anon., 2001

Going to war without France is like going deer hunting without your accordion.
  General Norman Schwarzkopf, commander of the
  Coalition Forces in the Gulf War

The only way the French are going in is if we tell them we found truffles in Iraq.
  Dennis Miller, American comedian and commentator

I don't know why people are surprised that France won't help us get Saddam out of Iraq. After all, France wouldn't help us get the Germans out of France!

Jay Leno

We can stand here like the French, or we can do something about it.

Marge Simpson, *The Simpsons*

President Bush is now launching an investigation into pre-war intelligence over weapons of mass destruction. If we find out that we were wrong, do we have to put Saddam Hussein back in the hole?

Jay Leno

This Iraqi intelligence scandal is growing. Americans are asking, 'What did President Bush not know?' and 'When did he mispronounce it?'

Craig Kilborn, late-night talk-show host

Bumper Stickers:

HOW DID OUR OIL GET UNDER THEIR SAND?
GO SOLAR, NOT BALLISTIC.
IT'S NUCLEAR, NOT NUCULAR, YOU IDIOT!
IT'S THE OIL, STUPID.
THE ONLY THING WE HAVE TO FEAR IS BUSH HIMSELF.
ANYTHING WAR CAN DO, PEACE CAN DO BETTER.
DROP BUSH, NOT BOMBS.
OH SAY CAN YOU CEASE?
DON'T DO IT, GEORGE, DAD WILL STILL LOVE YOU.
WAR IS SO LAST CENTURY.

See also: ARMY, OSAMA BIN LADEN, TONY BLAIR,
GEORGE W. BUSH, MILITARY, NUCLEAR WAR,
PEACE AND PACIFISM, WAR,

#IRELAND AND THE IRISH

The Irish are a fair people – they never speak well of one
another.
> Samuel Johnson, 1709–84, English poet, essayist and
> lexicographer

I showed my appreciation of my native land in the usual
Irish way by getting out of it as soon as I possibly could.
> George Bernard Shaw, 1856–1950, Irish playwright

Put an Irishman on the spit, and you can always get another
Irishman to turn him.
> George Bernard Shaw

We have always found the Irish a bit odd. They refuse to
be English.
> Winston Churchill (attrib.)

If, in the eyes of an Irishman, there is any one being more
ridiculous than an Englishman, it is an Englishman who
loves Ireland.
> André Maurois, 1885–1967, *Ariel*, 1923

My one claim to originality among Irishmen is that I never
made a speech.
> George Moore, 1852–1933, *Ave*, 1911

I never met anyone in Ireland who understood the Irish question, except one Englishman who had only been there a week.

Major Sir Keith Fraser, 1867–1935, British MP, 1919

The English and Americans dislike only *some* Irish – the same Irish that the Irish themselves detest, Irish writers – the ones that *think*.

Brendan Behan, 1923–64, *Richard's Cork Leg*, 1973

Michael's a statesman. His idea of danger is having an After Eight at 7.45.

Dublin voter quoted on Twitter, on Michael D. Higgins being elected as President of Ireland, October 2011

See also: BRITAIN AND THE BRITISH

J

#JOHNSON, BORIS, FORMER CONSERVATIVE MP AND MAYOR OF LONDON

I'm motivated 30 per cent by public service, 40 per cent by sheer egomania and 30 per cent by disapproval of swank-pot journalists.
   Boris Johnson

My position on cake is pro-having it, and pro-eating it.
   Boris Johnson

Some readers will no doubt say that a devil is inside me; and though my faith is a bit like Magic FM in the Chilterns, in that the signal comes and goes, I can only hope that isn't so.
   Boris Johnson, *Daily Telegraph*, 2004

I'm backing David Cameron's campaign out of pure, cynical self-interest.
   Boris Johnson during the Conservative Party leadership
   campaign, 2005

So why did Mr Johnson win? Some will put it down to his charisma, others to a poor choice of Labour candidate, but it's important not to underestimate the value of Mr

Johnson's hair. People always joke about it, but rarely do they grasp its significance. Its messiness invites voters' trust. They look at it and think, 'A man incapable of combing his hair is incapable of political scheming.' His chaotic bumbling suggests innocence, honesty.

> Michael Deacon, *Daily Telegraph*, 2012, reflecting on Boris Johnson's victory in the Mayoral elections

And how long have you been cutting your own hair?

> David Letterman, in an interview with Boris Johnson on *The Late Show*, June 2012

There was virtually only one thing safer than a bike hire stand in London. That was of course a bookshop.

> Boris Johnson on the London riots and looting of 2011

I have as much chance of becoming Prime Minister as of being decapitated by a frisbee or of finding Elvis.

> Boris Johnson, 2003

See also: LOCAL GOVERNMENT

#JOHNSON, LYNDON B., 1908–73, 36TH PRESIDENT OF THE UNITED STATES, 1963–69

I seldom think of politics more than eighteen hours a day.

> Lyndon B. Johnson

Johnson's instinct for power is as primordial as a salmon's going upstream to spawn.

> Theodore H. White, 1915–86, *The Making of the President*, 1964

I don't want loyalty. I want *loyalty*. I want him to kiss my ass in Macy's window at high noon and tell me it smells like roses. I want his pecker in my pocket.

Lyndon B. Johnson, discussing a prospective White House assistant

He's a man of his most recent word.

William F. Buckley Jr, 1925–2008, American conservative commentator

I have learned that only two things are necessary to keep one's wife happy. First, let her think she's having her own way. And second, let her have it.

Lyndon B. Johnson

It's probably better to have him inside the tent pissing out, than outside the tent pissing in.

Lyndon B. Johnson on FBI Director J. Edgar Hoover, 1971

When things haven't gone well for you, call in a secretary or a staff man and chew him out. You will sleep better and they will appreciate the attention.

Lyndon B. Johnson

Hyperbole was to Lyndon Johnson what oxygen is to life.

Bill Moyers, journalist and White House Press Secretary under Lyndon B. Johnson

When Lyndon Johnson wanted to persuade you of something, you really felt as if a St Bernard had licked your face for an hour.

Benjamin C. Bradlee, Executive Editor of the *Washington Post*

Light at the end of the tunnel? We don't even have a tunnel; we don't even know where the tunnel is.
  Lyndon B. Johnson

See also: PRESIDENCY, WHITE HOUSE

#JUSTICE

Injustice is relatively easy to bear; what stings is justice.
  H. L. Mencken, 1880–1956, American essayist and critic

Unless justice be done to others, it will not be done to us.
  Woodrow Wilson, 1856–1924, 28th President of the United
  States, 1913–21

See also: DEATH PENALTY, LAW

K

#KENNEDY, JOHN F., 1917-63, 35TH PRESIDENT OF THE UNITED STATES, 1961-63

I am one person who can truthfully say, 'I got my job through the *New York Times*.
  John F. Kennedy

Jack was out kissing babies while I was out passing bills. Someone had to tend the store.
  Lyndon B. Johnson, 1908–73, 36th President of the United States, 1963–69, Vice President under JFK

The enviably attractive nephew who sings an Irish ballad for the company and then winsomely disappears before the table-clearing and dish-washing begin.
  Lyndon B. Johnson

You can always tell a Harvard man, but you can't tell him much.
  Dwight D. Eisenhower, 1890–1969, 34th President of the United States, 1953–61

His speaking style is pseudo-Roman: 'Ask not what your country can do for you ...' Why not say, 'Don't ask...'? 'Ask not...' is the style of a man playing the role of being President, not of a man being President.

Herb Gold, *New York Post*, 1962

Everyone's talking about how young the candidates are. And it's true. A few months ago Kennedy's mother said, 'You have a choice ... do you want to go to camp this year or run for President?'

Bob Hope, 1903–2003, American comedian, during the Kennedy/Nixon Presidential campaign, 1960

I just received the following wire from my generous Daddy: 'Dear Jack, Don't buy a single vote more than is necessary. I'll be damned if I'm going to pay for a landslide.'

John F. Kennedy, during Presidential campaign

See also: PRESIDENCY, WHITE HOUSE

L

#LABOUR PARTY, THE

The worker's flag is deepest pink
It's not as red as people think
The old, the sick, the poor, the young
We will attack the weakest ones
And just to keep our conscience clear
We'll sing the Red Flag once a year.
　　Leon Rosselson, British folk singer; other versions available

If Labour is the answer, it must have been a bloody silly question.
　　Graffito, reported in *Daily Telegraph*, 1979

... reminding us ... of the Labour Party's enduring commitment to resentment and the general, surly feeling that we are always being done by anyone in the remotest position of authority.
　　Frank Johnson, 1943–2006, *The Times*, 1984

The Labour Party is like a stage coach. If you rattle along at great speed, everybody inside is too exhilarated or too seasick to cause any trouble. But if you stop, everybody gets out and argues about where to go next.
　　Harold Wilson, 1916–95, Labour Prime Minister, 1964–70,
　　1974–76, reported by Anthony Sampson, 1982

The longest suicide note in history.
  Gerald Kaufman, Labour MP, on the Labour Party General
  Election manifesto, 1983

It must never be forgotten that, whatever they say, the
things that divide the [Labour] party are much greater than
the things that unite it.
  Frank Johnson, *The Times*, 1981

I do not often attack the Labour Party. They do it so well
themselves.
  Edward Heath, 1916–2005, Conservative leader, speech,
  1973

I know that the right kind of political leader for the Labour
Party is a desiccated calculating machine.
  Aneurin Bevan, 1897–1960, Welsh Labour politician

The Labour Party Marxists see the consequences of their
own folly all around them and call it the collapse of
capitalism.
  Jon Akass, 1933–90, *The Sun,* 1976

I did not enter the Labour Party forty-seven years ago to have
our manifesto written by Dr Mori, Dr Gallup and Mr Harris.
  Tony Benn, Labour Minister

I don't support any organised party. I vote Labour.
  Anon.

We know what happens to people who stay in the middle of
the road. They get run over.
  Aneurin Bevan, debating the direction of his party after its
  electoral defeat in 1951

... that bunch of rootless intellectuals, alien Jews and international pederasts who call themselves the Labour Party.
  Alan Bennett, *Forty Years On*, 1968

My New Year's resolution is to find where the Labour Party
has been buried and the Tomb of the Unknown Socialist.
  Austin Mitchell, Labour MP

... they are not fit to manage a whelk stall.
  Winston Churchill, 1874–1965, British statesman, orator
  and writer (attrib.)

The only leaders Labour loves are dead ones.
  Robert Harris, British journalist and author

New Labour

Voting for New Labour is like helping an old lady across
the road while screaming, 'Get a move on!' Even the Tories,
who you could once rely on to be completely heartless, are
pretending to care.
  Boy George, British entertainer

New Labour did not invent lying, but they have raised it to
the status of high art.
  David Mellor, Conservative Cabinet minister

A few nights ago the Parliamentary Labour Party gathered for a slap-up feed in the Strangers' Dining Room,
Westminster. It was the first PLP dinner for ages.

'We stopped them holding them in the Blair–Brown years because we didn't trust each other with the knives,' says a comrade.
   Quentin Letts, *Daily Mail*, June 2012

See also: ED BALLS AND YVETTE COOPER, TONY BLAIR, GORDON BROWN, COMMUNISM, EQUALITY, LEFT, LEFT V. RIGHT, MARXISM, SOCIALISM

#LAW, THE

A lawyer with a briefcase can steal more than a hundred men with guns.
   Mario Puzo, 1920–99, Italian-American author and screenwriter

In law, nothing is certain but the expense.
   Samuel Butler, 1835–1902, English novelist

Distrust all men in whom the impulse to punish is powerful.
   Friedrich Nietzsche, 1844–1900, German philosopher

Charlie [advised to get a lawyer]: How much?
Babish: Assuming you saw nothing wrong, heard nothing wrong and did nothing wrong... about $100,000.
   Aaron Sorkin, *The West Wing*, 2001

The United States is a nation of laws, badly written and randomly enforced.
   Frank Zappa, 1940–93, composer and rock musician

I know no method to secure the repeal of bad or obnoxious laws so effective as their stringent execution.

>Ulysses S. Grant, 1822–85, Civil War commander and 18th President of the United States, 1869–77

Everyone in public life should be arrested at least once. It's an education.

>Alan Clark, 1928–99, Conservative MP and diarist

Nor do I propose to defend the right to talk on a mobile while driving a car, though I don't believe that is necessarily any more dangerous than the many other risky things that people do with their free hands while driving – nose-picking, reading the paper, studying the A–Z, beating the children, and so on.

>Boris Johnson, Conservative Mayor of London

Leo: There's two things in the world you never want to let people see how you make 'em: laws and sausages.

>Aaron Sorkin, *The West Wing*, 1999

See also: JUSTICE

#LEADERSHIP

The art of leadership is saying no, not yes. It is very easy to say yes.

>Tony Blair, Labour Prime Minister, 1997–2007, *Mail on Sunday*, 1994

As a political leader you start at your least capable and most popular. You end at your most capable and least popular.
    Tony Blair, at the Leveson Inquiry, 2012

No party is as bad as its leaders.
    Will Rogers, 1879–1935, American commentator and humorist

It is a fine thing to command, even if it only be a herd of cattle.
    Miguel de Cervantes, 1547–1616, *Don Quixote*, 1605

The disdain that political leaders show the ordinary citizen is reciprocated.
    Barry Sussman, American political analyst

Leadership is the ability to decide what is to be done and then to get others to want to do it.
    Dwight D. Eisenhower, 1890–1969, 34th American President, 1953–61

The task of the leader is to get his people from where they are to where they have not been.
    Henry Kissinger, American diplomat

Perhaps one of the most important accomplishments of my administration has been minding my own business.
    Calvin Coolidge, 1872–1933, 30th President of the United States, 1923–29

Everyone wants my blood, but no one wants my job.
    Guy Mollet, 1905–75, Socialist Prime Minister of France, 1956–57

The greatest leaders throughout history have been notoriously poor followers.
    Kathryn Collins, American writer

If you're not afraid to face the music, you may someday lead the band.
    Fred Metcalf for Sir David Frost, 1997

Charlatanism, to some degree, is indispensable to effective leadership.
    Eric Hoffer, 1902–83, American philosopher

The trouble with being a leader today is that you can't be sure if the people are following you or chasing you.
    Sir David Frost, showbiz veteran, 1997

A political leader must keep looking over his shoulder all the time to see if the boys are still there. If they aren't still there, he's no longer a political leader.
    Bernard Baruch, 1870–1965, American businessman, philanthropist and Presidential advisor

When the best leader's work is done, the people say, 'We did it ourselves.'
    Lao-tzu, philosopher and central figure in Chinese culture, possibly mythical

I must follow the people. Am I not their leader?
    Benjamin Disraeli, 1804–81, writer and Conservative Prime Minister, 1874–80

Since a politician never believes what he says, he is always astonished when others do.
    Charles de Gaulle, 1890–1970, French general and states-
    man and First President of the Fifth Republic, 1959–69

Politics is the ability to forecast what is going to happen tomorrow, next week, next month and next year. And to have the ability afterwards to explain why it didn't happen.
    Winston Churchill

It is hard to look up to a leader who keeps his ear to the ground.
    James H. Boren, 1925–2010, humorist and academic

Leadership appears to be the art of getting others to do something you are convinced should be done.
    Vance Packard, 1914–96, American journalist, critic
    and author

It's a terrible thing when you look over your shoulder when you are trying to lead – and to find no one there.
    Franklin D. Roosevelt, 1882–1945, 32nd President of the
    United States, 1933–45

We can't all be heroes because somebody has to sit on the curb and clap as they go by.
    Will Rogers

Only one man in a thousand is a leader of men – the other 999 follow women.
    Groucho Marx, 1890–1977, American comedian and actor

Either lead, follow or get out of the way.
    Sign on businessman Ted Turner's desk

We have leadership – there's just no followership.
George Danielson, 1915–98, US Democratic Congressman

A smile for a friend and a sneer for the world is the way to govern mankind.
Benjamin Disraeli

Leadership involves finding a parade and getting in front of it.
John Naisbitt, American futurist and writer

I believe in benevolent dictatorship, provided I am the dictator.
Richard Branson, British businessman

I must follow them; I am their leader.
Alexandre Auguste Ledru-Rollin, 1807–74, French politician

See also: PRESIDENCY

#LEFT, THE

One of the many problems with the American left, and indeed of the American left, has been its image and self-image as something rather too solemn, mirthless, herbivorous, dull, monochrome, righteous and boring.
Christopher Hitchens, 1949–2011, frontpagemag.com 2004

All Reformers, however strict their social conscience, live in houses just as big as they can pay for.
Logan Pearsall Smith, 1865–1946, *Afterthoughts*, 1931

The Good Samaritan for Sociologists

A man was attacked and left bleeding in a ditch. Two sociologists passed by and one said to the other, 'We must find the man who did this – he needs help.'
    Anon.

The word 'conservative' is used by the BBC as a portmanteau word of abuse for anyone whose views differ from the insufferable, smug, sanctimonious, naïve, guilt-ridden, wet pink orthodoxy of that sunset home of the third-rate minds of that third-rate decade, the 1960s.
    Norman Tebbit, Conservative politician, *The Independent*, 1990

The idiot who praises with enthusiastic tone,
All centuries but this and every country but his own ...
    W. S. Gilbert, *The Mikado*, 1885

See also: COMMUNISM, LABOUR PARTY, LEFT V. RIGHT, MARXISM, SOCIALISM, SOCIALISM V. COMMUNISM

#LEFT V. RIGHT

As Americans, we must ask ourselves: Are we really so different? Must we stereotype those who disagree with us? Do we truly believe that ALL red-state residents are ignorant racist fascist knuckle-dragging NASCAR-obsessed cousin-marrying roadkill-eating tobacco juice-dribbling gun-fondling religious fanatic rednecks; or that ALL blue-state residents are godless unpatriotic pierced-nose Volvo-driving France-loving left-wing communist

latte-sucking tofu-chomping holistic-wacko neurotic vegan weenie perverts?
   Dave Barry, *Miami Herald*

EVERY TIME YOU VOTE DEMOCRAT
GOD KILLS A KITTEN
   Bumper sticker

... further to the right than a fish-knife.
   Rod Liddle, of James Delingpole, *The Spectator*, 2011

See also: COMMUNISM, FASCISM, LABOUR PARTY, THE LEFT, MARXISM, SOCIALISM, SOCIALISM V. CAPITALISM

#LIBERAL DEMOCRATS, THE

The Lib Dems are not just empty. They are a void within a vacuum surrounded by a vast inanition.
   Boris Johnson, *Daily Telegraph*, 2003

Few organisations can debate for three days whether to stage a debate, hold the debate, have a vote and then proceed to have a debate about what they have debated. But that is why the Liberal Democrats hold a special place in the British constitution.
   Patrick Wintour, *The Guardian*, March 2012, discussing
   NHS reform at their Spring Conference

Like him or not, it's pretty certain that when they come to write the history of progressive liberal politics, Nick Clegg will buy a copy.
   Simon Blackwell, tweet, 2012

That is the sad problem with the Liberal Democrats: they always go for the middle way. It was once pointed out that if Christopher Columbus had been a Liberal Democrat, he'd probably have been content with discovering the mid-Atlantic.

Sir Malcolm Rifkind, House of Commons, 2012

A 'senior Liberal Democrat source' has been quoted in the papers as saying that, if the Conservatives vote down the reform, 'this will have consequences'. A threat by a Lib Dem! How terrifying! How macho! One shudders to think what form it will take. Perhaps each Tory rebel will awake to find a My Little Pony's head in his bed.

Michael Deacon, *Daily Telegraph*, 2012

I acknowledge that many Lib Dems have their hearts in the right place. But why does that place always have to be on their sleeves? Pious self-righteousness leaves me cold...

Tom Harris, Scottish Labour MP, Young Fabians blog, 2011

#LIBERAL PARTY, THE

As usual the Liberals offer a mixture of sound and original ideas. Unfortunately, none of the sound ideas is original and none of the original ideas is sound.

Harold Macmillan, 1894–1986, Conservative Prime
Minister, 1957–63, speech to London Conservatives, 1961

Attacking the Liberals is a difficult business, involving all the hazards of wrestling with a greased pig at a fair and then insulting the vicar.

Chris Patten, Conservative Cabinet minister

See also: LIB DEMS, LIBERALS AND LIBERALISM, LIBERAL PARTY, LIBERALS V. CONSERVATIVES, LEFT, LEFT V. RIGHT

#LIBERALS AND LIBERALISM

Liberal institutions straightaway cease from being liberal the moment they are soundly established.
  Friedrich Nietzsche

I can remember way back when a liberal was one who was generous with his own money.
  Will Rogers

I'm more of a man than any liberal.
  Ann Coulter, American commentator and controversialist

Usually the nonsense liberals spout is kind of cute, but in wartime their instinctive idiocy is life-threatening.
  Ann Coulter

Whether they are defending the Soviet Union or bleating for Saddam Hussein, liberals are always against America. They are either traitors or idiots.
  Liberals love America like O. J. loved Nicole.
  Ann Coulter

A liberal is a man too broadminded to take his own side in a quarrel.

Robert Frost, 1874–1963, American writer and poet

Liberals are just as fearful as reactionaries. For every 'Disgusted of Tunbridge Wells', there's a 'Horrified of Hampstead'.

Julie Burchill, British columnist and commentator

If liberals were prevented from ever again calling Republicans dumb, they would be robbed of half their arguments. To be sure, they would still have 'racist', 'fascist', 'homophobe', 'ugly', and a few other highly nuanced arguments in the quiver. But the loss of 'dumb' would nearly cripple them.

Ann Coulter, *Slander*, 2002

The radical of one country is the conservative of the next. The radical invents the views. When he has worn them out, the conservative adopts them.

Mark Twain, *Notebook*, 1935

The principal feature of American liberalism is sanctimoniousness. By loudly denouncing all bad things – war and hunger and date rape – liberals testify to their own terrific goodness. More important, they promote themselves to membership in a self-selecting elite of those who care deeply about such things... It's a kind of natural aristocracy, and the wonderful thing about this aristocracy is that you don't have to be brave, smart, strong or even lucky to join it, you just have to be liberal.

P. J. O'Rourke, *Give War a Chance*, 1992

At the core of liberalism is the spoiled child – miserable, as all spoiled children are, unsatisfied, demanding, ill-disciplined, despotic and useless. Liberalism is a philosophy of sniveling brats.
  P. J. O'Rourke, *Give War a Chance*, 1992

I have often been called a Nazi, and, although it is unfair, I don't let it bother me. I don't let it bother me for one simple reason. No one has ever had a fantasy about being tied to a bed and sexually ravished by someone dressed as a liberal.
  P. J. O'Rourke, *Give War a Chance*, 1992

A liberal is a conservative who's been mugged by reality.
  Anon.

What the liberal really wants is to bring about change that will not in any way endanger his position.
  Stokely Carmichael, 1941–98, American civil rights activist

A liberal is someone who feels a great debt to his fellow man, which debt he proposes to pay off with your money.
  G. Gordon Liddy, Watergate conspirator and now radio talk-show host

Bigot: a Conservative winning an argument with a Liberal.
  T-shirt slogan, Los Angeles 2009

A liberal is a man who leaves the room when the fight begins.
  Heywood Broun, 1888–1939, American newspaper columnist and editor

A liberal is someone who has enemies right and left.
  Anon.

A rich man told me recently that a liberal is a man who tells other people what to do with their money.

LeRoi Jones, *Home*, 1966

The second item in the liberal creed, after self-righteousness, is unaccountability. Liberals have invented whole college majors – Psychology, Sociology, Women's Studies – to prove that nothing is anybody's fault.

P. J. O'Rourke, libertarian journalist and commentator, 1992

... if God had been a Liberal, we wouldn't have had the Ten Commandments. We'd have the Ten Suggestions.

Malcolm Bradbury and Christopher Bigsby, *The After Dinner Game*, BBC TV, 1975

Liberalism: the haunting fear someone, somewhere, can help themselves.

Slogan on mug, Maine, 2009

WE CAN'T ALL BE LIBERALS.
SOME OF US HAVE TO WORK.

Bumper sticker, Texas, 2010

PROUD TO BE EVERYTHING
THE RIGHT WING HATES!

Bumper sticker, Washington, 2009

See also: LIB DEMS, LIBERALS AND LIBERALISM, LIBERAL PARTY, LIBERALS V. CONSERVATIVES, LEFT, LEFT V. RIGHT

#LIBERALS V. CONSERVATIVES

Liberals feel unworthy of their possessions. Conservatives feel they deserve everything they've stolen.
    Mort Sahl, American stand-up comedian

If you're not a liberal when you're twenty-five, you have no heart. If you're not a conservative by the time you're thirty-five, you have no brain.
    Winston Churchill (*Very* attrib.)

A radical is a man with both feet firmly planted in the air. A conservative is a man with two perfectly good legs who, however, has never learned to walk forward. A reactionary is a somnambulist walking backwards...
    Franklin D. Roosevelt, 'Fireside Chat', 1939

I said to my Liberal friend that we are fundamentally the same. I spend money like it's my money and you spend money like it's my money.
    Richard K. Armey, Republican Congressman, *Firing Line*,
    PBS 1990

Lord, help me to be the Conservative Liberals think I am.
    A Conservative's Prayer, Houston 2010

I'm liberal on some issues and conservative on others. For example, I would not burn a flag but neither would I put one out.
    Garry Shandling, American actor and comedian

... liberals protect themselves from detection with wild calumnies against anybody who opposes them. They have no interest in – or aptitude for – persuasion. Their goal is to anathematise their enemies.
Ann Coulter, 2007

See also: DEMOCRATS V. LIBERALS, LIB DEMS, LIBERALS AND LIBERALISM, LIBERAL PARTY, LEFT, LEFT V. RIGHT

#LIBERTARIANISM

Libertarianism is the philosophy which says that you can run your life better than the government can, and you have the right to be left alone in order to do it.
Anon.

There once was a man from Nantucket,
Who wanted to sell me a bucket,
But he could not, because,
There were too many laws,
So he threw up his hands and said, 'Vote Libertarian!'
Anon.

How many libertarians does it take to screw in a light bulb? None. The free market will handle it.
Anon.

If you are not free to choose wrongly and irresponsibly, you are not free at all. Jacob Hornberger, American libertarian, 1995

Libertarianism holds out, not the goal of a perfect society, but of a better and freer one. It promises a world in which more of the decisions will be made in the right way by the right person: you.

   David Boaz, *Libertarianism: A Primer*, 1997

I am hard put to find something to say to people who still think libertarianism has something to do with liberty. A libertarian is just a Republican who takes drugs.
Bob Black, *The Libertarian as Conservative*, 1984

A wise and frugal government which shall restrain men from injuring one another, which shall leave them otherwise free to regulate their own pursuits of industry and improvement, and shall not take from the mouth of labor the bread it has earned. This is the sum of good government.

   Thomas Jefferson, 1743–1826, 3rd President of the United

   States, 1801–09, 1801

It is much more important to kill bad bills than to pass good ones.

   Calvin Coolidge

If you have ten thousand regulations, you destroy all respect for the law.

   Winston Churchill

See also: CONSERVATIVES, REPUBLICANS, TEA PARTY

#LIBERTY

Liberty is the one thing you can't have unless you give it to others.
 William Allen White, 1868–1944, American author and politician

Liberty doesn't work as much in practice as it does in speeches.
 Will Rogers

Liberty means responsibility. That is why most men dread it.
 George Bernard Shaw, 1856–1950, Irish playwright

Liberty is always dangerous, but it's the safest thing we have.
 Harry Emerson Fosdick, 1878–1969, American clergyman

#LIES AND LYING

I welcome the opportunity of pricking the bloated bladder of lies with the poniard of truth.
 Aneurin Bevan, replying to a House of Commons speech by Winston Churchill

I should think it hardly possible to state the opposite of the truth with more precision.
 Winston Churchill, replying to a House of Commons speech by Aneurin Bevan

The Right Honourable gentleman is indebted to his memory for his jests and to his imagination for his facts.
 Richard Brinsley Sheridan, 1751–1816, English playwright, orator and statesman

[When asked if the press reports about an issue were reliable:] First they lie, then they re-lie, so I guess that makes them reliable.

> Abraham Lincoln, 1809–65, 16th President of the United
> States, 1861–65

If the Republicans will stop telling lies about the Democrats, we will stop telling the truth about them.

> Adlai Stevenson, 1900–1965, Governor of Illinois,
> Democratic Presidential Candidate 1952 and 1956

A lie is an abomination unto the Lord and a very present help in trouble.

> Adlai Stevenson

Every word she writes is a lie, including 'and' and 'the'.

> Mary McCarthy, 1912–89, American novelist, of Lillian
> Hellman, American author of plays and memoirs, *The Dick
> Cavett Show*, 1979

It is not a lie; it is a terminological inexactitude.

> Alexander Haig, 1924–2010, US Army General and states-
> man, defending himself against accusations of lying in 1983

A lie can be halfway round the world before the truth has got its boots on.

> James Callaghan, 1912–2005, Labour Prime Minister,
> 1976–79; not original

It contains a misleading impression, not a lie. It was being economical with the truth.

> Sir Robert Armstrong, British life peer and former civil
> servant. Quote from the *Spycatcher* trial, 1986

... economical with the *actualité* ...
> Alan Clark, admission of withholding the truth while a
> government minister answering questions in Parliament,
> 1992

I am not accusing Mrs Thatcher of lying. I am merely
suggesting she has what psychologists call, 'selective
amnesia'.
> Denis Healey, Labour Chancellor of the Exchequer, 1974–79

It's the inherent right of the government to lie to save itself.
> Arthur D. Sylvester, American Assistant Secretary of
> Defense, 1962

A little inaccuracy sometimes saves tons of explanation.
> Saki, 1870–1916, *The Square Egg*, 1924

The short memories of American voters is what keeps our
politicians in office.
> Will Rogers

There is a great deal of hard lying in the world; especially
among people whose characters are above suspicion.
> Benjamin Jowett, 1817–93, theologian and scholar (attrib.)

It is hard to believe that a man is telling the truth when you
know that you would lie if you were in his place.
> H. L. Mencken, 1880–1956, American essayist and critic

There is some truth in the media's claim that politicians are
lying bastards.
> Bernard Ingham, formerly press secretary to Margaret
> Thatcher

We all know that Prime Ministers are wedded to the truth, but like other married couples they sometimes live apart.
   Saki, *The Unbearable Bassington*, 1912

President Bartlet: Two politicians are having an argument. One of them stands up and says, 'You're lying!' The other one answers, 'Yes, I am, but hear me out.'
   Aaron Sorkin, *The West Wing*, 2000

See also: TRUTH

#LINCOLN, ABRAHAM, 1809–65, 16TH PRESIDENT OF THE UNITED STATES, 1861–65

From time to time, life as a leader can look hopeless. To help you, consider a man who lived through this: Failed in business at age thirty-one. Defeated for the legislature at thirty-two. Again failed in business at thirty-four. Sweetheart died at thirty-five. Had a nervous breakdown at thirty-six. Defeated in election at thirty-eight. Defeated for Congress at forty-three. Defeated for Congress at forty-six. Defeated for Congress at forty-eight. Defeated for Senate at fifty-five. Defeated for Vice President at fifty-six. Defeated for Senate at fifty-eight. Elected President at age sixty. This man was Abraham Lincoln.
   Chicago Times, editorial following the Gettysburg Address,
   1863 (attrib.)

Were it not for my little jokes, I could not bear the burdens of this office.
   Abraham Lincoln

... is a filthy storyteller, despot, liar, thief, braggart, buffoon, usurper, monster, ignoramus, old scoundrel, perjurer, robber, swindler, tyrant, field-butcher, land-pirate.
     Harper's Weekly, 1860

... is a first-rate second-rate man ... a mere convenience waiting like any other broomstick to be used.
     Wendell Phillips, 1811–84, American orator, abolitionist and social reformer

Apart from that, Mrs Lincoln, how did you enjoy the play?
     Tom Lehrer, American lyricist and entertainer

If I were two-faced, would I be wearing this one?
     Abraham Lincoln

See also: PRESIDENCY, WHITE HOUSE

#LLOYD GEORGE, DAVID, 1863–1945, LIBERAL POLITICIAN AND PRIME MINISTER 1916–22

He can't see a belt without hitting below it.
     Margot Asquith, 1864–1945, Anglo-Scottish socialite and wit

I always knew Lloyd George won the war but until I read his memoirs, I didn't know he'd done it single-handedly.
     Margot Asquith

Lloyd George was a wonderful orator. I have heard my father say that when he came to address meetings in Scotland you had to hold on to your seat not to be carried away.
     Jennie Lee, 1904–1988, Labour peer, wife of Aneurin Bevan

He spoke for 117 minutes, in which period he was detected only once in the use of an argument.
Arnold Bennett, 1867–1931, English novelist and playwright

This extraordinary figure of our time, this siren, this goat-footed bard, this half-human visitor to our age from the hag-ridden magic and enchanted woods of Celtic antiquity.
John Maynard Keynes, 1883–1946, *Essays in Biography*, 1933

He did not seem to care which way he travelled as long as he was in the driving seat.
Lord Beaverbrook,1879–1964, *The Decline and Fall of Lloyd George*, 1963

He aroused every feeling except trust.
A. J. P. Taylor, 1906–90, historian

… the Happy Warrior of Squandermania.
Winston Churchill, debate in the House of Commons on the 1929 Budget

See also: LIBERALS AND LIBERALISM

#LOCAL GOVERNMENT

It is now known that men enter local politics solely as a result of being unhappily married.
C. Northcote Parkinson, *Parkinson's Law*, 1957

State legislators are merely politicians whose darkest secret prohibits them from running for high office.

Dennis Miller, American stand-up and political commentator
Asking a town hall to slim down its staff is like asking an alcoholic to blow up a distillery. Antony Jay and Jonathan Lynn, *Yes Minister*, 1980

See also: BUREAUCRACY, GOVERNMENT

M

#MACDONALD, RAMSAY, 1866–1937, FIRST EVER LABOUR PRIME MINISTER, 1929–35

He has, more than any other man, the gift of compressing the largest amount of words into the smallest amount of thought.
    Winston Churchill, 1874–1965, British statesman, orator
    and writer

... I have waited fifty years to see the boneless wonder sitting on the Treasury Bench.
    Winston Churchill, speech to the House of Commons,
    1931

... sufficient conscience to bother him but not sufficient to keep him straight.
    David Lloyd George, 1863–1945, Liberal Prime Minister,
    1916–22

See also: LABOUR PARTY

#MACMILLAN, HAROLD, 1894-1986, CONSERVATIVE POLITICIAN AND PRIME MINISTER, 1957-63

Forever poised between a cliché and an indiscretion.
> Harold Macmillan's description of the role of Foreign
> Secretary, *Newsweek* magazine, 1956

The Prime Minister has an absolute genius for putting flamboyant labels on empty luggage.
> Aneurin Bevan, 1897–1960, Welsh Labour Cabinet minister, speech to the House of Commons

The arch mediocrity who presided, rather than ruled, over a Cabinet of mediocrities ... not a statesman, a state-monger. Pre-emptory on little questions, the great ones he left open.
> Harold Wilson, 1916–95, Labour Prime Minister, 1964–70,
> 1974–76, in 1961

See also: CONSERVATIVE PARTY, CONSERVATIVES AND CONSERVATISM

#MAJOR, SIR JOHN, CONSERVATIVE PRIME MINISTER, 1990-97

My New Year's resolution? To stay cool, calm and elected.
> Fred Metcalf for John Major, in conversation with David
> Frost, BBC1, January 1997

... the man who ran away from the circus to become an accountant.
> Anon.

... so unpopular, if he became a funeral director people would stop dying.
Tony Banks, 1942–2006, Labour MP and Cabinet minister

I was looking for a wine to suit my palate. So I went into Google and typed 'dry, white, smooth yet sparkling'.
And up came John Major!
Sally Poplin, English humorous writer

I am walking over hot coals suspended over a deep pit at the bottom of which are a large number of vipers baring their fangs.
John Major

See also: CONSERVATIVE PARTY, CONSERVATIVES AND CONSERVATISM

#MAJORITY

A majority is always the best repartee.
Benjamin Disraeli, 1804–81, writer and Conservative
Prime Minister, 1874–80

Whenever you find that you are on the side of the majority, it is time to reform.
Mark Twain, 1835–1910, American writer and humorist

The test of courage comes when we are in the minority. The test of tolerance comes when we are in the majority.
Ralph W. Sockman, 1889–1970, American writer and
preacher

The majority, compose them how you will, are a herd and not a very nice one.
William Hazlitt, 1778–1830, English essayist and critic

When great changes occur in history, when great principles are involved, as a rule, the majority are wrong.
Eugene V. Debs, 1855–1926, American socialist and trades union leader

See also: ELECTIONS, VOTING

#MARXISM

Je suis Marxiste – tendance Groucho.
Slogan, Paris, 1968

Marxists are people whose insides are torn up day after day because they want to rule the world and no one will even publish their letter to the editor.
Mark Helprin, American novelist

I could go for Marxism as long as it meant overthrowing a junta, but I don't want to live under it.
Roy Blount Jr, *Playboy*, 1983

M is for Marx
And Movement of Masses
And Massing of Arses
And Clashing of Classes
Cyril Connolly, 'Where Engels Fears to Tread', 1945

All I know is that I am not a Marxist.
  Karl Marx, 1818–93, German philosopher and revolutionary socialist, quoted by Friedrich Engels (attrib.)

Why does the Marxist only drink herbal tea?
Because all proper tea is theft.
  Anon.

Among artists without talent Marxism will always be
popular, since it enables them to blame society for the fact
that nobody wants to hear what they have to say.
  Clive James, Australian poet and critic, *Daily Telegraph*, 2012

Like Johnson's friend, Edwards, I too have tried to be a
Marxist but common sense kept breaking in.
  A. J. P. Taylor, 1906–90, British historian, *Journal of*
  Modern History, 1977

There was an old Marxist called Lenin
Who did two or three million men in.
That's a lot to have done in,
But where he did one in,
That grand Marxist, Stalin, did ten in.
  Robert Conquest, English poet and historian

See also: COMMUNISM, CUBA, EQUALITY, LABOUR
PARTY, LEFT V. RIGHT, LEFT, SOCIALISM V.
CAPITALISM, SOCIALISM

#MILIBAND, ED, LEADER OF THE LABOUR PARTY, 2010–

I may be new to this game, but I think I ask the questions.
  Ed Miliband, at his first Prime Minister's Questions as
  Leader of the Opposition, 2010

Ed Miliband has an unerring ability to sniff out a trap, and then stride straight into it. He's like a mouse with a death wish.
  Michael Deacon, *Daily Telegraph*, November 2011

Mr Miliband threw up his hands imploringly. He looked like a zit-speckled teenager pleading with his girlfriend not to dump him. At any moment I expected him to burst into a rendition of Badfinger's distraught break-up ballad, 'Without You'. 'I can't liiiive, if living is without yoo-oo-ou. Can't liiiiiiiiiive, I can't give any mooooore ...'
  Michael Deacon, *Daily Telegraph*, January 2012, describing Miliband's speech in Scotland on Scottish independence

... Ed Miliband has now gone – what? – three or four days without a crisis... For the time being, the Labour leader doesn't look a total calamity. Keep this up for another week or two and he may even reach the heady heights of mediocrity.
  Michael Deacon, *Daily Telegraph*, February 2012

I suppose not everyone has a dad who wrote a book saying he didn't believe in the parliamentary road to socialism.
  Ed Miliband

#MILITARY, THE

War is much too serious a thing to be left to military men.
  Charles de Talleyrand, 1754–1838, French diplomat at the
  time of Louis XVI, Napoleon and the French Revolution

Military intelligence is a contradiction in terms.
  Groucho Marx, 1890–1977, American comedian and actor

A good general not only sees the way to victory, he also
knows when victory is impossible.
  Polybius, c. 200–118 BC, Greek historian of the Hellenistic
  period

We spend so much money on the military, yet we're slash-
ing education budgets throughout the country. No wonder
we've got smart bombs and stupid fucking children.
  Jon Stewart, American comic and commentator

A politician is a fellow who will lay down your life for his
country.
  Texas Guinan, 1878–1933, American saloon-keeper and
  actress

See also: ARMY, DEFENCE, IRAQ WAR, NUCLEAR WAR,

#MISTAKES

I am humble enough to recognise that I have made mistakes,
but politically astute enough to have forgotten what
they are.
  Michael Heseltine, Conservative Cabinet minister

It is fatal in life to be right too soon.
   Enoch Powell, 1912–98, Conservative politician and author

To err is human. To blame someone else is politics.
   Hubert Humphrey, 1911–78, Democratic Vice President
   under Lyndon B. Johnson

#MONEY

Money is like manure. You have to spread it around or
it smells.
   J. Paul Getty, 1892–1976, American industrialist

Money is better than poverty, if only for financial reasons.
   Woody Allen, *Without Feathers*, 1972

Money is like a sixth sense without which you cannot make
a complete use of the other five.
   W. Somerset Maugham, 1874–1965, *Of Human Bondage*,
   1915

Money can't buy friends but you can get a better class
of enemy.
   Spike Milligan, 1918–2002, *Puckoon*, 1963

Money is something you have to make in case you don't die.
   Sally Poplin

See also: BANKS AND BANKING, BIG BUSINESS, BUSINESS, CAPITALISM, CREDIT CRUNCH, ECONOMICS AND ECONOMISTS, ECONOMY, INFLATION, POVERTY, RICH AND POOR, STOCK MARKET AND WALL STREET, TAXATION, WEALTH

#MULTICULTURALISM

As one is always obliged to explain when tiptoeing around this territory, I am not a racist, only a culturist. I believe Western culture – rule of law, universal suffrage – is preferable to Arab culture. That's why there are millions of Muslims in Scandinavia, and four Scandinavians in Syria.

    Mark Steyn, Canadian author and columnist, 2002

The great thing about multiculturalism is it doesn't involve knowing anything about other cultures – the capital of Bhutan, the principal exports of Malawi, who cares? All it requires is feeling good about other cultures. It's fundamentally a fraud, and I think was subliminally accepted on that basis. Most adherents to the idea that all cultures are equal don't want to live in anything but an advanced Western society.

    Mark Steyn, 2006

The deal with multiculturalism is that the only culture you're allowed to disapprove of is your own.

    Martin Amis, English novelist

See also: WAR ON TERROR

N

#NATIONALISM

A nation is a society united by a delusion about its ancestry
and a common hatred of its neighbours.
  William R. Inge, 1860–1954, English author and Dean of
  St Paul's Cathedral

Nationalism is an infantile disease. It is the measles of
mankind.
  Albert Einstein, 1879–1955, German physicist

I love my country too much to be a nationalist.
  Albert Camus, 1913–1960, French author, journalist and
  philosopher

See also: PATRIOTISM

#NEW ZEALAND

A country of inveterate, backwoods, thick-headed, egotistic
philistines.
  Vladimir Ilich Lenin, 1870–1924, Russian Marxist revolutionary and political theorist, 1909

If an English butler and an English nanny sat down to design a country, they would come up with New Zealand.
    Sally Poplin, English humorous writer

New Zealand was colonised initially by those Australians who had the initiative to escape.
    Robert Muldoon, 1921–92, 31st Prime Minister of New Zealand, 1981

The United States has Ronald Reagan, Bob Hope, Johnny Cash and Stevie Wonder. New Zealand has Robert Muldoon, no hope, no cash and no wonder!
    Anon.

'TERRIBLE TRAGEDY OF THE SOUTH SEAS. THREE MILLION PEOPLE TRAPPED ALIVE.'
    Tom Scott, New Zealand writer, apocryphal headline, 1979

He's probably been detained by a full-length mirror.
    David Lange, 1942–2005, Labour Prime Minister of New Zealand, of Winston Peters, founder of the New Zealand First Party

#NEWSPAPERS

See: THE PRESS

#NIXON, RICHARD, 1913-94, 90TH PRESIDENT OF THE UNITED STATES, 1969-74

Would you buy a used car from this man?
> Campaign slogan used against Nixon, 1968

Richard Nixon is a no-good, lying bastard. He can lie out of both sides of his mouth at the same time, and if he ever caught himself telling the truth, he'd lie just to keep his hand in.
> Harry S. Truman, 1884–1972, 33rd President of the United
> States, 1945–53

Richard Nixon inherited some good instincts from his Quaker forebears but, by diligent hard work, he overcame them.
> James Reston, 1909–95, American journalist

... a naïve, inept, maladjusted Throttlebottom.
> Emanuel Celler, 1888–1981, American Democratic politician

Nixon just isn't half the man Hitler was.
> Richard Dudman, chief of *St Louis Post Dispatch*,
> Washington bureau

Solutions are not the answer.
> Richard Nixon

Let's face it, there's something perversely endearing about a man so totally his own worst enemy that even achieving the presidency was merely something he had to do in order to be able to lose it.
> Paul Slansky, American writer

He is the kind of politician who would cut down a redwood tree and then mount the stump to make a speech for conservation.
>   Adlai Stevenson, 1900–1965, Governor of Illinois,
>   Democratic Presidential Candidate 1952 and 1956, in 1956

Nixon's motto was, 'If two wrongs don't make a right, try three.'
>   Norman Cousins, 1915–90, American academic and
>   journalist

... it is quite extraordinary! He will even tell a lie when it is not convenient to. That is the sign of a great artist ...
>   Gore Vidal, 1925–2012, interviewed on *Russell Harty Plus*,
>   London Weekend Television, 1972

President Nixon was so crooked that he needed servants to help him screw his pants on in the morning.
>   Hunter S. Thompson, 1937–2005, author and Gonzo
>   journalist

The trouble with Nixon is that he's a serious politics junkie. He's totally hooked and like any other junkie, he's a bummer to have around, especially as President.
>   Hunter S. Thompson

... the integrity of a hyena and the style of a poison toad.
>   Hunter S. Thompson

... a Main Street Machiavelli.
>   Patrick Anderson, 1915–79, Canadian poet

Watergate

He told us he was going to take crime out of the streets. He did. He took it into the damn White House.
　　Rev. Ralph D. Abernathy, 1926–90, minister and civil rights leader

Richard Nixon means never having to say you're sorry.
　　Wilfrid Sheed, 1930–2011, *GQ*, 1984

I'm a fan of President Nixon. I worship the quicksand he walks on.
　　Art Buchwald, 1925–2007, American humorous commentator, 1974

[Presidential Press Secretary] Ron Ziegler has done for government credibility what the Boston Strangler did for door-to-door salesmen.
　　Art Buchwald

This we learn from Watergate,
That almost any creep'll
Be glad to help the government
Overthrow the people.
　　E. Y. Harburg, 1896–1981, *At this Point in Rhyme*, 1976

See also: PRESIDENCY, WHITE HOUSE

#NORTH KOREA

The administration says that taking military action against North Korea all depends on whether or not their plutonium has any oil.

Craig Kilborn, late-night talk-show host

Last week North Korea publicly admitted for the first time it has nuclear weapons. The Bush administration has so far shown very little concern, as the North Korean missiles are believed only capable of reaching the Blue States.

Jon Stewart, American comic and commentator

America has had to deal with eccentric dictators in the past: Idi Amin, Muammar Gaddafi, Ming the Merciless ... but now the security of the world is threatened by Kim Jong Il, a nerdy, pompadoured, platform shoe-wearer who looks like something you'd put on the end of your child's pencil.

Jon Stewart

President Bush met with the President of South Korea. Things got off to an awkward start when President Bush asked, 'Are you from the good Korea or the bad Korea?'

Conan O'Brien, late-night talk-show host

Kim Jong Il, the crazy leader of North Korea who hate us, passed away over the weekend. And get this – his 28-year-old son, Kim Jong Un, is taking over. It won't be easy. He's got some big women's sunglasses to fill.

Jimmy Fallon, late-night talk-show host, 2012

North Korean leader Kim Jong Un has been awarded the highest rank in the country's military. The decision was praised by everyone from parliamentary leader Kim Jong Un to opposition leader Kim Jong Un.

Conan O'Brien, 2012

See also: COMMUNISM, CUBA, SOCIALISM

#NUCLEAR WEAPONS

The best way not to use nuclear weapons is to be prepared to use them.

Samuel S. Stratton, 1916–90, Democratic Representative for New York for nearly thirty years

No annihilation without representation!

Arnold J. Toynbee, 1889–1975, British historian

The way to win an atomic war is to make certain it never starts.

Omar Bradley, 1893–1981, American General and Chairman of the Joint Chiefs of Staff

The Atomic Age is here to stay – but are we?

Bennet Cerf, 1898–1971, American editor, publisher and TV panellist

You're an old-timer if you can remember when 'setting the world on fire' was a figure of speech.

Franklin P. Jones, 1908–80, American author and lawyer

When you've seen one nuclear war, you've seen them all.

T-shirt, London, 1986

Toby: Why's a test-ban treaty so important? Let me tell you. In 1974, India set off a peaceful nuclear explosion. Indira Gandhi herself said they had no intention of building a bomb, they just wanted to know that they could. Twenty years later India sets off five nuclear explosions. Who gets nervous? Pakistan. And when Pakistan gets nervous, everybody get nervous. You know why? 'Cause we're all gonna die.

    Aaron Sorkin, *The West Wing*, 2000

See also: ARMY, MILITARY, WAR

O

#OBAMA, BARACK, 44TH PRESIDENT OF THE UNITED STATES, 2008–

Who is Barack Obama? Contrary to the rumours you have heard, I was not born in a manger. I was actually born on Krypton and sent here by my father Jor-El to save the Planet Earth.

Many of you know that I got my name, Barack, from my father. What you may not know is Barack is actually Swahili for 'That One'. And I got my middle name from somebody who obviously didn't think I'd ever run for President.

If I had to name my greatest strength, I guess it would be my humility. Greatest weakness, it's possible that I'm a little too awesome.

Barack Obama, speaking at Alfred E. Smith Memorial Foundation Dinner, New York, 2008

The good news is that, according to the Obama administration, the rich will pay for everything. The bad news is that, according to the Obama administration, you're rich.

P. J. O'Rourke, libertarian journalist and commentator

I'LL KEEP MY FREEDOM, MY GUNS AND MY MONEY. YOU CAN KEEP THE CHANGE!

Republican Election Bumper sticker

CONTRARY TO WHAT YOU'VE BEEN TAUGHT
NOBODY OWES YOU A THING!
    Republican Bumper sticker

YES, WICCAN!
    Bumper sticker

President Obama met the Queen of England, and gave her
an iPod as a gift. When British Prime Minister Gordon
Brown was here, Obama gave him a DVD box set. So,
it looks like he's saving the big gift, the Nintendo, for
the Pope.
    Jay Leno, late-night talk-show host

President Obama, whose instinctive reaction to pretty much
everything that happens, including sunrise, is to deliver a
nationally televised address...
    Dave Barry, *Miami Herald*, 2011

Police in Texas seized a shipment of ecstasy pills this week
shaped like President Obama's face. The drug is charac-
terised by a brief powerful high followed by a long, slow
comedown.
    Seth Meyers, *Saturday Night Live*, 2010

In the State of the Union address, President Obama calls on
Congress to improve the nation's crumbling infrastructure.
He is interrupted seventy-nine times by applause, and four
times by falling chunks of the Capitol ceiling.
    Dave Barry, *Miami Herald*, 2011

The Jonas Brothers are here ... Sasha and Malia are huge fans. But boys, don't get any ideas!
I have two words for you: Predator Drones.
Barack Obama, White House Correspondents' Dinner, Washington, 2010

We're fighting three wars now. Imagine how many we'd be fighting if President Obama hadn't won the Nobel Peace Prize.
Jay Leno, commenting on American involvement in Libya, 2011

President Obama took Michelle out to a steak restaurant for her birthday, marking the first time in months the words 'Obama' and 'well done' appeared in the same sentence.
Jimmy Fallon, late-night talk-show host, 2012

A man wearing an Obama mask robbed a bank. Either that or Obama has an exciting new plan to reduce the deficit.
Conan O'Brien, late-night talk-show host

President Obama's approval ratings are so low now, Kenyans are accusing him of being born in the United States.
Jay Leno, 2011

It's an honour to be here. If you'd told me as a kid, I would be sitting on the same dais as President Barack Obama, I would have said, 'The President's name is Barack Obama?'
Jimmy Kimmel, White House Correspondents' Dinner, 2012

Mr President, remember when the country rallied behind you in the hopes of a better tomorrow?
That was hilarious!
Jimmy Kimmel, White House Correspondents' Dinner, 2012

You know, the real reason people thought you were from Kenya has nothing to do with your birth certificate. It's because you lost so much weight, we thought you were the guy who won the Boston Marathon.

This is how you know the country is in bad shape: the President is starving! North Korea is sending him food aid!

   Jimmy Kimmel

'If you've got a business, YOU didn't do it. Somebody ELSE made that happen,' said the man who stated that HE single-handedly killed bin Laden.

   Someecards, reacting to Obama's entrepreneur-bashing,
   July 2012

Jobless claims rose again by 35,000 last week. Not good. But it does show that if you're unsuccessful in this country, you didn't do it on your own. You had help. Thank you, President Obama.

   Jay Leno, reacting to Obama's entrepreneur-bashing, July
   2012

See also: DEMOCRATIC PARTY, DEMOCRATS, DEMOCRAT SLOGANS, PRESIDENCY, WHITE HOUSE

#OCCUPY MOVEMENT

This Occupy Wall Street movement is now in 1,500 places all around the world. I was at the Occupy Beverly Hills today. It's two Jews at Starbucks complaining that the scones aren't fresh, but still it's a start.

   Bill Maher, late-night talk-show host, 2011

The Occupy Wall Street protests continue to grow. They've started to attract a very unsavoury element – celebrities.
    Craig Ferguson, late-night talk-show host, 2011

The Occupy Wall Street protesters gathered outside Rupert Murdoch's house chanting, 'What do we want?' Murdoch interrupted saying, 'I already know, I hacked your phones.'
    Craig Ferguson

Over the weekend, a group of Occupy Wall Street protesters tried to reoccupy a New York park. You can tell the movement has been hurting for funds. This time they called themselves 'Occupy Wall Street brought to you by Sony Pictures' 21 *Jump Street*.'
    Conan O'Brien, 2012

I love the protests. And if you think about it, what better way to send a message to Wall Street than by sitting in a pup tent banging on a drum.
    David Letterman, late-night talk-show host, 2012

The truth is the First Lady is right. Americans are in terrible shape. You can even tell how out of shape we are by the way we protest. We used to march. Now we occupy.
    Must say a quick congratulations to the Occupy protesters. It took months and months of patchouli oil and hacky sack but finally Wall Street isn't greedy any more. Congratulations!
    Jimmy Kimmel, 2012

See also: BANKS AND BANKING, PROTEST, REVOLUTION, SLOGANS, STOCK MARKET AND WALL STREET, TEA PARTY

#OIL

Now they're saying all this terrorist activity could lead to higher oil prices. When asked why, the oil companies said, 'Cause everything leads to higher oil prices'. In fact, the price of crude oil could hit $80 a barrel. That's not crude – that's obscene.

    Jay Leno, 2006

Congress just passed a law against gas station price-gauging. You know how you can tell if a gas station is price-gauging? If the sign says 'Open'.

    Jay Leno, 2007

In Louisiana, BP claims that it's making progress with the leaking oil in the Gulf. They're working on a plan to heat the Gulf up to 600 degrees and use it to fry chicken.

    Jimmy Kimmel, 2010

British Petroleum said today that if this spill gets worse, they may soon have to start drilling for water.

    David Letterman, 2010

Officials at BP have filed for permits to drill for oil again in the Gulf of Mexico. They say the oil is easier to find than ever because it's mostly on top of the water.

    Conan O'Brien, 2011

See also: ENVIRONMENT

#OPPOSITION

No government can be long secure without a formidable Opposition.

> Benjamin Disraeli, 1804–81, *Coningsby*, 1844

In Parliament it should not only be the duty but the pleasure of the opposition to oppose whenever they reasonably can.

> Iain Macleod, 1913–70, Conservative Cabinet minister

The duty of an opposition is very simple: to oppose everything and propose nothing.

> Lord Derby, 1865–1948, British soldier, politician and diplomat

Opposition is four or five years' humiliation in which there is no escape from the indignity of no longer controlling events.

> Roy Hattersley, British Labour politician and journalist

See also: ENEMIES

P

#PALIN, SARAH, ALASKAN GOVERNOR AND REPUBLICAN VICE PRESIDENTIAL CANDIDATE

It's like a really bad Disney movie. The hockey mom, you know, 'Oh, I'm just a hockey mom'... and she's facing down President Putin... It's totally absurd ... it's a really terrifying possibility... I need to know if she really thinks that dinosaurs were here 4,000 years ago. I want to know that, I really do. Because she's gonna have the nuclear codes.
   Matt Damon, actor

Being politicians, they all got to sharing their personal stories. Obama talked about his mother's battle with cancer. Harry Reid talked about a kid with a cleft palate. And John McCain told how he once carried a braindead woman through an entire campaign.
   Bill Maher, late-night talk-show host, on Obama's health
   care summit

Sarah Palin's new autobiography doesn't come out until November, but it is already No. 1 on Amazon. And if you go to the website, it says, 'People who bought this book also bought no other books in their entire life.'
   Jimmy Fallon, late-night talk-show host

A new study says that radiation from wi-fi is hurting trees. Environmentalists are calling it the worst assault on trees since George W. Bush and Sarah Palin became authors.

Jimmy Fallon

Now how about this, ladies and gentlemen? The Governor of Alaska, Sarah Palin, has announced she is stepping down. She will no longer be the Governor of Alaska. First thing, she woke up and went out on her porch and waved goodbye to Russia.

David Letterman, late-night talk-show host

John McCain said that Sarah Palin is still a force in the Republican Party. Then he got in his car and backed over his mailbox.

David Letterman

Sarah Palin's book is big, 400 pages. She wrote the book herself and agonised over every word, and so will you.

David Letterman

I wish Sarah Palin was an Apple product so that she would be completely obsolete in six months.

Someecards, 2011

This was all part of that hope and change and transparency. Now, a year later, I gotta ask the supporters of all that, 'How's that hopey, changey stuff working out?'

Sarah Palin, at the National Tea Party Convention, 2010, following America's experience of Obama's promised 'Hope and Change'

It's just so great to be back on Fox News, a network that both pays me and shows me the questions ahead of time. I just hope that tonight the lamestream media won't twist my words by repeating them verbatim.
  Tina Fey as Sarah Palin, *Saturday Night Live*, 2011

See also: REPUBLICAN PARTY, TEA PARTY

#PATRIOTISM

Patriotism is the last refuge of a scoundrel.
  Samuel Johnson, 1709–84, English poet, essayist and
  lexicographer

Patriotism is a kind of religion. It is the egg from which wars are hatched.
  Guy de Maupassant, 1850–93, French writer of short stories

Patriotism is the willingness to kill and be killed for trivial reasons.
  Bertrand Russell, 1872–1970, British philosopher, historian
  and social critic

An author's first duty is to let down his country.
  Brendan Behan, 1923–64, Irish playwright, *The Guardian*,
  1960

In the beginning of a change, the patriot is a scarce man, and brave and hated and scorned. When his cause succeeds the timid join him, for then it costs nothing to be a patriot.
  Mark Twain, *Notebooks*, 1935

Patriotism is your conviction that this country is superior to all other countries because you were born in it.
George Bernard Shaw, 1856–1950, Irish playwright

Patriotism is often an arbitrary veneration of real estate over principle.
George Jean Nathan, 1882–1958, American editor and drama critic

Patriotism has become a mere national assertion, a sentimentality of flag-cheering with no constructive duties.
H. G. Wells, 1866–1946, British science fiction writer

Patriotism is the virtue of the vicious.
Oscar Wilde, 1854–1900, Irish playwright

Patriotism is as fierce as a fever, pitiless as the grave, blind as a stone and as irrational as a headless man.
Ambrose Bierce, 1842–1913, *The Devil's Dictionary*, 1911

'My country, right or wrong' is a thing no patriot would think of saying except in a desperate case. It is like saying, 'My mother, drunk or sober'.
G. K. Chesterton, 1874–1936, *The Defendant,* 1901

The less a statesman amounts to, the more he loves the flag.
Kin Hubbard, 1868–1930, American cartoonist, humorist and journalist

When I am abroad, I always make it a rule never to criticise or attack the government of my own country. I make up for lost time when I come home.
Winston Churchill, 1874–1965, British statesman, orator and writer (attrib.)

See also: NATIONALISM

#PEACE AND PACIFISM

Sometime they'll give a war and nobody will come.
　　Carl Sandburg, 1878–1967, Pulitzer Prize winning writer,
　　poet and editor

Peace, n. In international affairs, a period of cheating between two periods of fighting.
　　Ambrose Bierce, *The Devil's Dictionary*, 1911

Again and again we have owed peace to the fact that we were prepared for war.
　　Theodore Roosevelt, 1858–1919, 26th President of the
　　United States, 1901–09

Peace is not only better than war, but infinitely more arduous.
　　George Bernard Shaw

A bayonet is a weapon with a worker at each end.
　　British pacifist slogan, Second World War

Join the Army, see the world, meet interesting people – and kill them.
　　Pacifist badge, 1978

It's coexistence
Or no existence.
　　Bertrand Russell

Gone are those pleasant nineteenth-century days when a country could remain neutral and at peace just by saying it wanted to.

William Shirer, 1904–93, American journalist and historian

#POLITICAL CORRECTNESS

Political correctness means always having to say you're sorry.

Slogan on mug, Exeter, 2011

Open discussion of many major public questions has for some time now been taboo. We can't open our mouths without being denounced as racists, misogynists, suprema-cists, imperialists or fascists. As for the media, they stand ready to trash anyone so designated.

Saul Bellow, 1915–2005, American novelist

It's easy to be politically correct and a liberal when you live in a gated community.

Bobcat Goldthwait, American comedian

The perfect representative on a government committee is a disabled black Welsh woman trades unionist.

Antony Jay and Jonathan Lynn, *Yes Minister*, 1980

Three blind mice walk into a pub. But they are all unaware of their surroundings, so to derive humour from it would be exploitative.

Bill Bailey, British comedian

Dean Kagan, distinguished faculty, parents, friends, gradu-
ating seniors, Secret Service Agents, class agents, people of
class, people of colour, colourful people, people of height, the
vertically constrained, people of hair, the differently coiffed,
the optically challenged, the temporarily sighted, the insight-
ful, the out-of-sight, the out-of-towners, the Eurocentrics,
the Afrocentrics, the Afrocentrics with Eurailpasses, the
eccentrically inclined, the sexually disinclined, people of
sex, sexy people, sexist pigs, animal companions, friends
of the earth, friends of the boss, the temporarily employed,
the differently employed, the differently optioned, people
with options, people with stock options, the divestiturists,
the deconstructionists, the home constructionists, the home
boys, the homeless, the temporarily housed at home, and,
God save us, the permanently housed at home.
  Garry Trudeau, cartoonist, opening of speech at Yale
  University Class Day, 1999

It is an article of passionate faith among 'politically correct'
biologists and anthropologists that brain size has no
connection with intelligence; that intelligence has nothing
to do with genes; and that genes are probably nasty fascist
things anyway.
  Richard Dawkins, scientist and author, *The Economist*,
  1993

C. J.: Okay, but I've got to be careful about saying 'man'.
Toby: Why, because–? Oh, c'mon!
C. J.: You'd be surprised. I get letters.
Toby: Fine, 'human being', then, or do the other mammals
complain?
  Paul Redford, *The West Wing*, 2003

See also: MULTICULTURALISM

#POLITICAL PARTIES

There's no way in the world you're going to make a political party respectable unless you keep it out of office.
  Will Rogers, 1879–1935, American commentator and humorist

See also: CONSERVATIVE PARTY, LABOUR PARTY, LIB DEMS, LIBERAL PARTY, DEMOCRATIC PARTY, REPUBLICAN PARTY

#POLITICIANS

He gave it for his opinion, that whosoever could make two ears of corn or two blades of grass to grow upon a spot of ground where only one grew before, would deserve better of mankind, and do more essential service to his country, than the whole race of politicians put together.
  Jonathan Swift, 1667–1745, *Gulliver's Travels*, 1726

Successful democratic politicians are insecure and intimidated men. They advance politically only as they placate, appease, bribe, seduce, bamboozle or otherwise manage to manipulate the demanding and threatening elements in their constituencies.
  Walter Lippmann, 1889–1974, *The Public Philosophy*, 1955

Sometimes I wonder whether the world is being run by smart people who are putting us on, or by imbeciles who really mean it.
  Mark Twain, 1835–1910, American writer and humorist

A politician is a person with whose politics you don't agree; if you agree with him he's a statesman.
  David Lloyd George, 1863–1945, Liberal Prime Minister, 1916–22

Politics are too serious a matter to be left to the politicians.
  Charles de Gaulle, 1890–1970, French general and statesman and First President of the Fifth Republic, 1959–69

Mothers all want their sons to grow up to be President, but they don't want them to become politicians in the process.
  John F. Kennedy, 1917–63, 35th President of the United States, 1961–63

Being an MP feeds your vanity and starves your self-respect.
  Matthew Parris, former Conservative MP, *The Times*, 1994

We pretend to be thick-skinned, we candidates, but there is one thing that makes us blush to the roots. What we hate, what we fear, is being ignored.
  Boris Johnson, Conservative Mayor of London

He knows nothing and he thinks he knows everything. That points clearly to a political career.
  George Bernard Shaw, *Major Barbara*, 1905

Politicians are interested in people. Not that this is always a virtue. Fleas are interested in dogs.
  P. J. O'Rourke, libertarian journalist and commentator

Ninety-eight per cent of the adults in this country are decent, hard-working, honest Americans. It's the other lousy 2 per cent that get all the publicity. But then – we elected them.

   Lily Tomlin, American comedian

Bureaucrats want bigger bureaus. Special interests are interested in whatever's special to them. These two groups bring great pressure to bear upon politicians who have another agenda yet: to cater to the temporary whims and fads of the public and the press.

   P. J. O'Rourke, *All the Trouble in the World*, 1994

Public office is the last refuge of the scoundrel.

   Boies Penrose, 1860–1921, American lawyer and
   Republican politician

In order to become the master, the politician poses as the servant.

   Charles de Gaulle

To be a successful politician you've got to be able to sit on the fence while keeping both ears to the ground.

   Anon.

Too bad the only people who know how to run the country are busy driving cabs or cutting hair.

   George Burns, 1896–1996, American comedian

Men play at being God but lacking God's experience, they wind up as politicians.

   Harry William King, American wit

The most successful politician is he who says what everybody is thinking most often and in the loudest voice.
Theodore Roosevelt

Politicians are the same all over. They promise to build a bridge even when there is no river.
Nikita Krushchev, 1894–1971, Russian leader, speaking to reporters, New York, 1960

Now and then an innocent man is sent to the legislature.
Kin Hubbard

A statesman is a successful politician who is dead.
Thomas B. Reed, 1839–1902, Speaker of the US House of Representatives

Now I know what a statesman is; he's a dead politician. We need more statesmen.
Bob Edwards, radio journalist

A statesman is any politician it's considered safe to name a school after.
Bill Vaughan, 1915–77, American journalist and columnist

The public say they are getting cynical about politicians. They should hear how politicians talk about them.
George Walden, journalist and Conservative MP

Ninety per cent of politicians give the other ten per cent a bad reputation.
Henry Kissinger, American diplomat

A politician should have three hats. One for throwing in the ring, one for talking through and one for pulling rabbits out of if elected.
   Carl Sandburg, 1878–1967, American poet and editor

Politics is not the art of the possible. It consists in choosing between the disastrous and the unpalatable.
   John Kenneth Galbraith, 1908–2006, Canadian-American economist

Any party which takes credit for the rain, must not be surprised if its opponents blame it for the drought.
   Dwight W. Morrow, 1873–1931, American businessman, diplomat and politician

Politicians are like children; you can't just give them what they want – it only encourages them.
   Antony Jay and Jonathan Lynn, *Yes, Prime Minister*, 1986

#POLITICS

Politics are for foreigners with their endless wrongs and paltry rights. Politics are a lousy way to get things done. Politics are, like God's infinite mercy, a last resort.
   P. J. O'Rourke

Stupidity got us here. It can get us out.
   Will Rogers

All politics is based on the indifference of the majority.
   James Reston, 1909–95, American author and journalist

Politics is like Hollywood for ugly people.
   Jay Leno, late-night talk-show host

He may be a son-of-a-bitch but he's *our* son-of-a-bitch.
   Franklin D. Roosevelt, 1882–1945, 32nd President of the
   United States, 1933–45, of President Somoza of Nicaragua,
   1938 (attrib.)

The whole aim of practical politics is to keep the populace alarmed (and hence clamorous to be led to safety) by menacing it with an endless series of hobgoblins, all of them imaginary.
   H. L Mencken, 1880–1956, American essayist and critic

Politics offers yesterday's answers to today's problems.
   Marshall McLuhan, 1911–80, Canadian educator and
   philosopher

Politics is the art of stopping people from minding their own business.
   José Ortega y Gasset, *Tel Quel*, 1943

In politics, you get what you deserve rather than what you want.
   Cecil Parkinson, Conservative Cabinet minister

I looked up 'politics' in the dictionary the other day. It's derived from two words: 'Poli' meaning 'many' and 'tics' meaning 'bloodsuckers'.
   Sally Poplin, English humorous writer

The first mistake in politics is the going into it.
> Benjamin Franklin, 1706–90, author, politician, satirist,
> musician, inventor and one of the Founding Fathers of the
> United States

I am unsuited to politics since I am unable to wish for or accept my opponent's death.
> Albert Camus, 1913–60, French author, journalist and
> philosopher

One aspect of politics too little acknowledged is that besides being jolly serious and all that, it is also a hugely enjoyable game for boys.
> Andrew Marr, author and BBC political interviewer

Greater love hath no man than this, that he lay down his friends for his political life.
> Jeremy Thorpe, Liberal MP, on Prime Minister Harold
> Macmillan's dramatic Cabinet reshuffle in which seven
> ministers were sacked, 1962

I did not become a politician because I could not stand the strain of having to be right all the time.
> Peter Ustinov, 1921–2004, British actor, writer, monologuist

Nothing is so admirable in politics as a short memory.
> John Kenneth Galbraith

Gratitude is not a normal feature of political life.
> Lord Kilmuir, 1900–1967, Conservative peer, *Political
> Adventure*, 1964

There are no true friends in politics. We are all sharks circling and waiting for traces of blood to appear in the water.

    Alan Clark, 1928–99, Conservative MP, *Diary*, 1990

Practical politics consists in ignoring facts.

    Henry Adams, 1838–1918, American journalist, novelist
    and historian

Being in politics is like being a football coach. You have to be smart enough to understand the game and dumb enough to think it's important.

    Eugene McCarthy, 1916–2005, American poet and politician

Politics is supposed to be the second oldest profession. I have come to realise that it bears a very close resemblance to the first.

    Ronald Reagan, 1911–2004, 40th President of the United
    States, 1981–89

Politics: a strife of interests masquerading as a conflict of principles. The conduct of public affairs for private advantage.

    Ambrose Bierce, 1842–1913, *The Devil's Dictionary*, 1911

In politics, as on the sickbed, people toss from one side to the other, thinking they will be more comfortable.

    Johann Wolfgang von Goethe, 1749–1832, German writer,
    artist and polymath

If you can't stand the heat, get out of the kitchen.

    Harry S. Truman, 1884–1972, 33rd President of the United
    States, 1945–53

Politics is the skilled use of blunt objects.

> Lester B. Pearson, 1897–1972, 14th Prime Minister of Canada, 1963–68, 1972

Politics, like music and golf, is best learned at an early age.

> Lawrence Welk, 1903–92, American bandleader and impresario, 1975

Politics is perhaps the only profession for which no preparation is thought necessary.

> Robert Louis Stevenson, 1850–94, Scottish novelist and essayist

I have learned that one of the most important rules of politics is poise – which means looking like an owl after you've behaved like a jackass.

> Ronald Reagan

Politics are almost as exciting as war and quite as dangerous. In war you can only be killed once but in politics, many times.

> Winston Churchill

'Practical politics' means selfish ends promoted by base means.

> Rutherford B. Hayes, 1822–93, 19th President of the United States, 1877–81

Politics is the art of preventing people from busying themselves with what is their own business.

> Paul Valéry, 1871–1945, French poet, essayist and philosopher

Nothing can be said about politics that hasn't already been said about haemorrhoids.
   Denis Leary, American actor, writer and comedian

One of the penalties for refusing to get involved in politics is that you end up being governed by your inferiors.
   Plato, 424–348 BC, Athenian philosopher

Politics is the art of postponing decisions until they are no longer relevant.
   Henri Queuille, 1884–1970, *The Bureaucrat*, 1985

#POVERTY

I've been rich and I've been poor; rich is better.
   Sophie Tucker, 1884–1966, American singer

Poverty is no disgrace to a man, but it is confoundedly inconvenient.
   Sydney Smith, 1771–1845, *His Wit and Wisdom*, 1900

America is an enormous frosted cupcake in the middle of millions of starving people.
   Gloria Steinem, American journalist, feminist and activist

Very few people can afford to be poor.
   George Bernard Shaw

I hate the poor and look forward eagerly to their extermination.
   George Bernard Shaw

The trouble with being poor is that it takes up all your time.
  Willem de Kooning, 1904–97, abstract artist

Lack of money is the root of all evil.
  George Bernard Shaw

There is only one class in the community that thinks more about money than the rich, and that is the poor. The poor can think of nothing else.
  Oscar Wilde, 'The Soul of Man under Socialism', 1891

Poverty is an anomaly to rich people. It is very difficult to make out why people who want dinner do not ring the bell.
  Walter Bagehot, 1826–77, English essayist, journalist and businessman

Look at me – I worked my way up from nothing to a state of extreme poverty.
  Groucho Marx, 1890–1977, American comedian and actor

I'm always amazed how the poor can take so much of our money and yet still remain poor. What are they doing with it?
  Greg Proops, American comedian

... is that a fairtrade banana in your pocket or are you just pleased to see me & conscious of farmhands' working conditions in Peru?
  blindfumble, tweet, 2012

See also: BANKS AND BANKING, BIG BUSINESS, BUSINESS, CAPITALISM, CREDIT CRUNCH, ECONOMICS AND ECONOMISTS, ECONOMY,

INFLATION, MONEY, RICH AND POOR, STOCK MARKET AND WALL STREET, TAXATION, WEALTH

#POWER

The way to have power is to take it.
> W. M. Tweed, 1823–78, notably corrupt New York politician

It is certainly more agreeable to have power to give than to receive.
> Winston Churchill

A friend in power is a friend lost.
> Henry Adams, 1821–91, *The Education of Henry Adams*, 1906

Seven months ago I could give a single command and 541,000 people would immediately obey it. Today I can't get a plumber to come to my house.
> Norman Schwarzkopf, retired US Army General, *Newsweek*, 1991

Power is the ultimate aphrodisiac.
> Henry Kissinger, quoted in *The Guardian*, 1976

Being powerful is like being a lady. If you have to tell people you are, you aren't.
> Margaret Thatcher, Conservative Prime Minister, 1979–90

#PRESIDENCY, THE AMERICAN

I sit here all day trying to persuade people to do the things they ought to have sense enough to do without my persuading them. That's all the powers of the President amount to.
  Harry S. Truman

All the President is, is a glorified public relations man who spends his time flattering, kissing and kicking people to get them to do what they are supposed to do anyway.
  Harry S. Truman, letter to his sister, 1947

Any man who has had the job I've had and didn't have a sense of humour wouldn't still be here.
  Harry S. Truman

The President is always abused. If he isn't, he isn't doing anything.
  Harry S. Truman

There's one thing about being President – no one can tell you when to sit down.
  Dwight D. Eisenhower, 1890–1969, 34th President of the United States, 1953–61

In America any boy may become President and I suppose it's just one of the risks he takes.
  Adlai Stevenson, 1900–65, Governor of Illinois,
  Democratic Presidential Candidate 1952 and 1956, speech,
  Indianapolis, 1952

When the President says, 'Jump,' they only ask, 'How high?'
> John Ehrlichman, 1925–99, counsel to the President for
> Domestic Affairs under Richard Nixon; key figure
> in Watergate

The power to blow up the world cannot be entrusted to anyone sick enough to seek it.
> Philip Slater, American actor, sociologist and writer

The US Presidency is a Tudor monarchy plus telephones.
> Anthony Burgess, 1917–93, English novelist

I would rather be right than President.
> Henry Clay, 1777–1852, American lawyer, politician
> and orator

A man who is influenced by the polls or is afraid to make decisions that may make him unpopular is not a man to represent the welfare of the country.
> Harry S. Truman

When a man has cast his longing eye on offices, a rottenness begins in his conduct.
> Thomas Jefferson, 1743–1826, 3rd President of the United
> States, 1801–09

Seen one President, you've seen them all.
> Henry Kissinger

Presidency, n. The greased pig in the field game of American politics.
> Ambrose Bierce, 1842–1913, *The Devil's Dictionary*, 1911

When I was a boy I was told that anybody could become President; I'm beginning to believe it.
> Clarence Darrow, 1857–1938, American lawyer, wit and civil libertarian

Once upon a time my political opponents honoured me as possessing the fabulous and intellectual power by which I created a worldwide depression all by myself.
> Herbert Hoover, 1874–1964, 31ˢᵗ President of the United States, 1929–33

No man will ever bring out of the Presidency the reputation which carries him into it.
> Thomas Jefferson

The Presidential system just won't work any more. Anyone who gets in under it ought not to be allowed to serve.
> Gore Vidal, 1925–2012, American writer and political commentator, 1980

I am a man of limited talents from a small town. I don't seem to grasp that I am President.
> Warren G. Harding, 1865–1923, 29ᵗʰ President of the United States, 1921–23

I felt as if I had lived five lifetimes in my first five days as President.
> Harry S. Truman

If forced to choose between the penitentiary and the White House for four years, I would say the penitentiary, thank you.
William T. Sherman, 1820–91, American educator and Civil War general

Oh, that lovely title, *ex*-President.
Dwight D. Eisenhower

If Presidents don't do it to their wives, they do it to the country.
Mel Brooks, American actor and comedy writer

Being President is like running a cemetery. You've got a lot of people under you and nobody's listening.
Bill Clinton, 42nd President of the United States, 1993–2001

I have a fantasy where [media mogul] Ted Turner is elected President but refuses because he doesn't want to give up power.
Arthur C. Clarke, 1917–2008, British science fiction author and futurist

If you are as happy, my dear friend, on entering this house as I am leaving it and returning home, you are the happiest man in this country.
James Buchanan Jr, 1791–1868, 15th President of the United States, 1857–61, in a message to his successor, Abraham Lincoln

You're asking the leader of the Western world a chicken-shit question like that?
> Lyndon B. Johnson, 1908–73, 36th President of the United States, 1963–69, to a reporter

The President is like being a jackass caught in a rainstorm. You've just got to stand there and take it.
> Lyndon B. Johnson

A President's hardest task is not to do what is right, but to know what is right.
> Lyndon B. Johnson

The pay is good, and I can walk to work.
> John F. Kennedy

In our brief national history we have shot four of our Presidents, worried five of them to death, impeached one and hounded another out of office. And when all else fails, we hold an election and assassinate their character.
> P. J. O'Rourke

The President of today is just the postage stamp of tomorrow.
> Gracie Allen, 1895–1964, American comedian

The President of the United States serves a minimum four-year sentence with no time off for good behaviour.
> Anon.

No one who has ever held the office of President would congratulate a friend on obtaining it.

    John Adams, 1735–1826, 2nd President of the United States, 1797–1801

When you get to be President, there are honours, the 21-gun salutes, all those things. You have to remember it isn't for you. It's for the President.

    Harry S. Truman

Study hard and you might grow up to be President. But let's face it, you'll never make as much money as your dog.

    George H. W. Bush, 1992, speech to graduates after learning that Millie, his dog, made $889,000 in a book deal

People think I sit here and push buttons and get things accomplished. Well, I spent today kissing behinds.

    Harry S. Truman

There are blessed intervals when I forget, by one means or the other, that I am President of the United States.

    Woodrow Wilson, 1856–1924, 28th President of the United States, 1913–21

My average of meeting with people was about eighty a day for eight years.

    Ronald Reagan

Everyone makes mistakes. Presidents just find out about them sooner.

When things go wrong, they like to blame the President, and that's one of the things that Presidents are paid for.
John F. Kennedy

Once a President gets to the White House, the only audience that really matters is history.
Doris Goodwin, American biographer and historian, *New York Times*

Within the first few months I discovered that being a President is like riding a tiger. A man has to keep riding or be swallowed.
Harry S. Truman

The American Presidency, it occurs to us, is merely a way-station en route to the blessed condition of being an ex-President.
John Updike, 1932–2009, American novelist

C. J.: Overwhelming response to the State of the Union. Thirty-six interruptions for applause.
President Bartlet: I don't know what's more embarrassing: that we count them or that I care.
Mark Goffman, *The West Wing*, 2005

The only President who didn't blame the previous administration for all his troubles was George Washington.
Anon.

See also individual Presidents
See also: VICE PRESIDENCY

#PRESS, THE

The man who reads nothing at all is better educated than the man who reads nothing but newspapers.
    Thomas Jefferson

Newspapers always excite curiosity. No one ever lays one down without a feeling of disappointment.
    Charles Lamb, 1775–1834, English essayist

A journalist is a grumbler, a censurer, a giver of advice, a regent of sovereigns, a tutor of nations. Four hostile newspapers are more to be feared than a thousand bayonets.
    Napoleon Bonaparte, 1769–1821, French Emperor

Journalism largely consists in saying 'Lord Jones Dead' to people who never knew Lord Jones was alive.
    G. K. Chesterton, *The Wisdom of Father Brown*, 1914

Cronyism is the curse of journalism. After many years I have reached the firm conclusion that it is impossible for any objective newspaperman to be a friend of a President.
    Walter Lippmann, 1889–1974, American intellectual,
    writer and political commentator

You cannot hope to bribe or twist,
thank God! the
British journalist.
But, seeing what
the man will do
unbribed, there's
no occasion to.
    Humbert Wolfe, 'Over the Fire'

Every President should have the right to shoot two reporters a year – without explanation.

Herbert Hoover

I hope we never live to see the day when a thing is as bad as some of our newspapers make it.

Will Rogers, 1934

[A device] unable ... to discriminate between a bicycle accident and the collapse of civilisation.

George Bernard Shaw, on 'the newspaper'

If a politician murders his mother, the first response of the press or of his opponents will likely be not that it was a terrible thing to do, but rather that in a statement made six years before he had gone on record as being opposed to matricide.

Meg Greenfield, 1930–99, *Washington Post* editorial writer

Once a newspaper touches a story, the facts are lost for ever, even to the protagonists.

Norman Mailer, 1923–2007, American novelist

All successful newspapers are ceaselessly querulous and bellicose. They never defend anyone or anything if they can help it; if the job is forced upon them, they tackle it by denouncing someone or something else.

H. L. Mencken, *Prejudices*, First Series, 1919

There are moments when we in the British press can show extraordinary sensitivity; these moments usually coincide with the death of a proprietor, or a proprietor's wife.
   Craig Brown, British satirist

The *New York Times* editorial page is like a ouija board that has only three answers, no matter what the question. The answers are: higher taxes, more restrictions on political speech and stricter gun control.
   Ann Coulter, American commentator and controversialist

Only the aspirants for President are fool enough to believe what they read in the newspapers.
   Christopher Hitchens, 1949–2011, British-American jour-
   nalist and controversialist, C-SPAN, 1988

The one function that TV news performs very well is that when there is no news, we give it to you with the same emphasis as if there was news.
   David Brinkley, 1920–2003, TV newscaster and journalist

Reading about one's failings in the daily papers is one of the privileges of high office in this free country of ours.
   Nelson A. Rockefeller, 1908–79, American businessman,
   philanthropist, Governor of New York and Vice President
   under Gerald Ford

Virginio Gayda is about the only newspaperman we know of who can write the way a peke barks.
   Frank Sullivan, 1892–1976, American journalist and
   humorist

If one morning I walked on top of the water across the Potomac River, the headline that afternoon would read 'President Can't Swim'.
Lyndon B. Johnson

Nobody believes a rumour here in Washington until it's officially denied.
Edward Cheyfitz, 1914–59, American labour attorney

Ministers do not believe they exist unless they are reading about themselves in the newspapers.
Antony Jay and Jonathan Lynn, *Yes Minister*, 1981

Newspaper editors are men who separate the wheat from the chaff, and then print the chaff.
Adlai Stevenson

Were it left to me to decide whether we should have a government without newspapers or newspapers without a government, I should not hesitate for a moment to prefer the latter.
Thomas Jefferson

I'm with you on the free press. It's the newspapers I can't stand.
Tom Stoppard, *Night and Day*, 1978

The difference between literature and journalism is that journalism is unreadable and literature is not read.
Oscar Wilde

We live under a government of men and morning newspapers.

Wendell Phillips, 1811–84, American abolitionist and orator

All the faults of the age come from Christianity and journalism.

Frank Harris, 1856–1931, Irish-American author, journalist
and publisher

There is only one way for a newspaperman to look at a politician and that is down.

Frank H. Simonds, American historian

Politicians who complain about the media are like ships' captains who complain about the sea.

Enoch Powell, 1912–98, Conservative politician (attrib.)

Freedom of the press is limited to those who own one.

A. J. Liebling, 1904–63, *New Yorker* journalist

The government is the only known vessel that leaks from the top.

James Reston

I do not take a single newspaper, nor read one a month, and I feel myself infinitely the happier for it.

Thomas Jefferson

People everywhere confuse
What they read in the newspapers with news.

A. J. Liebling

Any man with ambition, integrity – and ten million dollars – can start a daily newspaper.
Henry Morgan, 1915–94, American radio comedian

It is the newspaper's duty to print the news and raise hell.
Chicago Times, 1861

Never trust a smiling reporter.
Ed Koch, New York mayor

The morning paper is just as necessary for an American as dew is to the grass.
Josh Billings, 1818–85, American humorist

Lickspittle: a useful functionary, not infrequently found editing a newspaper.
Ambrose Bierce, 1842–1913, *The Devil's Dictionary*, 1911

Journalism consists of buying white paper at two cents a pound and selling it at ten cents a pound.
Charles A. Dana, 1819–1997, American philanthropist and journalist

Never lose your temper with the press or the public is a major rule of political life.
Christabel Pankhurst, 1880–1958, activist and suffragette

Never pick a fight with someone who buys his ink by the barrel.
Anon.

I read the newspapers avidly. It is my one form of continuous fiction.

> Aneurin Bevan, 1897–1960, Welsh Labour minister, interview, *The Times*, 1960

News expands to fill the time and space allocated to its coverage.

> William Safire, 1929–2009, American commentator

Jim Hacker: 'Don't tell me about the press. I know exactly who reads the papers:
The *Daily Mirror* is read by people who think they run the country;
The Guardian is read by people who think they ought to run the country;
The Times is read by people who actually do run the country;
The *Daily Mail* is read by the wives of the people who run the country;
The *Financial Times* is read by people who own the country;
The *Morning Star* is read by people who think the country ought to be run by another country;
And the *Daily Telegraph* is read by people who think it is.'
Sir Humphrey: 'Prime Minister, what about the people who read *The Sun*?'
Bernard Woolley: '*Sun* readers don't care who runs the country, as long as she's got big tits.'

> Antony Jay and Jonathan Lynn, *Yes, Prime Minister*, 1987

Only government can take perfectly good paper, cover it with perfectly good ink and make the combination worthless.

> Milton Friedman, 1912–2006, American economist

News is something that somebody wants suppressed. All the rest is advertising.

> William Randolph Hearst, 1863–1951, American newspaper publisher (attrib.)

It's amazing that the amount of news that happens in the world every day just exactly fits the newspaper.

> Jerry Seinfeld, American stand-up comic

Mr Humphrys has a unique genius for fault-finding. When Mr Cameron said he starts work at 5.45am, it was a surprise Mr Humphrys didn't find fault with that.

'Five forty-five, Prime Minister? Why not 5.40? Or, better yet, 5.35? What are you doing for those five or ten minutes that you deem more important than running the country?'

'Well, I'm brushing my teeth.'

'So, Prime Minister, you're telling us that the brightness of your smile matters more to the people of Britain than deporting terror suspects, cutting the deficit and creating jobs?'

'Well, no, but… Look, all right, from now on I'll start work at 5.35am.'

'Five thirty-five? Why not 5.30? Why not THE NIGHT BEFORE?'

> Michael Deacon, *Daily Telegraph*, 2012 imagining an interview between BBC Radio Four's John Humphrys and David Cameron

Newspaper readership is declining like crazy. In fact, there's a good chance that nobody is reading my column.

> Dave Barry, *Miami Herald*

95 per cent of news articles about shark attacks feature a picture of an entirely innocent shark.

> made-up stats, tweet, 2012

Daily Mail: Will Contaminated Vegetables Spreading Deadly E.Coli Through Europe Eventually Kill Every Last One of Us?
   No.
   Private Eye, 2011

See also: PROPAGANDA, TELEVISION

#PRIME MINISTER

Former Prime Ministers are like great rafts floating untethered in a harbour.
   William Ewart Gladstone, 1809–98, four-time Liberal
   Prime Minister

The first essential for a Prime Minister is to be a good butcher.
   William Ewart Gladstone

There are three classes that need sanctuary more than others – birds, wild flowers and Prime Ministers.
   Stanley Baldwin, 1867–1947, Conservative politician and
   three-time Prime Minister, *The Observer*, 1925

#PROPAGANDA

History is the propaganda of the victors.
   Ernst Toller, 1893–1939, German playwright and politician

... the propaganda arm of the American Dream machine, Hollywood ...

Molly Haskell, American feminist, film critic and author

The propagandist's purpose is to make one set of people forget that certain other sets of people are human.

Aldous Huxley, 1894–1963, English writer

See also: THE PRESS, TELEVISION

#PROTEST

In the whole range of human occupations is it possible to imagine a poorer thing to be than an iconoclast? It is the lowest of all the unskilled trades.

G. K. Chesterton, *Daily News*, 1905

Protest: when wrongs are rioted.

Anon.

The main accomplishment of nearly all organised protests is to annoy people who are not in them.

Dave Barry, *Miami Herald*

Non-violence is a flop. The only bigger flop is violence.

Joan Baez

We are the Folk Song Army,
Every one of us cares,
We all hate poverty, war and injustice
Unlike the rest of you squares.

Tom Lehrer, singer-songwriter, satirist, 'The Folk Song Army', 1965

It's not cricket to picket...
  Harold Rome, 1908–93, American composer and lyricist,
  song from *Pins and Needles*, 1937

I'm against picketing but I don't know how to show it.
  Mitch Hedberg, 1968–2005, American comedian

Agitators are a set of interfering meddling people, who come
down to some perfectly contented class of the community
and sow the seeds of discontent among them. That is the
reason why agitators are so absolutely necessary.
  Oscar Wilde, 'The Soul of Man under Socialism', 1891

Q

#QUAYLE, DAN, VICE PRESIDENT OF THE UNITED STATES UNDER GEORGE H. W. BUSH

Dan Quayle taught the kids a valuable lesson: if you don't study, you could wind up as Vice President.

Jay Leno, late-night talk-show host

Quaylisms:

- The President is going to lead us out of this recovery.
- I stand by all the mis-statements I've made.
- A zebra cannot change its spots.
- If we don't succeed, we run the risk of failure.
- We're going to have the best-educated American people in the world.
- The trend towards democracy is inevitable – but it can be stopped.
- We are not ready for an unforeseen event that may or may not occur.
- We must expect them (Salvadorian officials) to work toward the elimination of human rights.
- It is wonderful to be here in the great state of Chicago.

See also: GEORGE H. W. BUSH, VICE PRESIDENCY

R

#RACE

There are many humorous things in the world, among them the white man's notion that he is less savage than other savages.
  Mark Twain, 1835–1910, American writer and humorist

Wouldn't it be a hell of a thing if all this was burnt cork and you people were being tolerant for nothing?
  Dick Gregory, black comedian, *Nigger*, 1965

We should be thankful to lynch mobs. I've got a brother who can run a half-mile faster than any white boy in the world.
  Dick Gregory

I say violence is necessary. It is as American as cherry pie.
  H. Rap Brown, black activist, 1967

Racial prejudice is a pigment of the imagination.
  Sally Poplin, English humorous writer

I'm a WASP – a White Anglo-Saxon Protestant – and actually, a lot of my people are doing *really* well.
  Penelope Lombard, American stand-up comic

Now, if you're average and *white*, honey, you can go far. Just look at Dan Quayle. If that boy was colored, he'd be washing dishes somewhere.

    Annie Elizabeth Delang, *Having Our Say*, 1992

I think racism is a terrible thing. I think we should all learn to hate each other on an individual basis.

    Cathy Ladman, Jewish-American actor and comedian

The trouble with the Jews is they are just like everyone else. Only more so.

    Jackie Mason, American stand-up comedian

The modern definition of 'racist' is 'someone who is winning an argument with a liberal'.

    Peter Brimelow, British American author, financial journalist and paleoconservative

A black man failing black history ... ain't that some sad shit ... cuz you *know*, fat people don't fail cooking!

    Chris Rock, *Bring the Pain*, HBO, 1996

If it wasn't for Abe, I'd still be on the open market.

    Dick Gregory, on Abraham Lincoln

There's a lot of racism going on. Who's more racist, black people or white people? It's black people! You know why? Because we hate black people too! Everything white people don't like about black people, black people *really* don't like about black people and there's two sides, there's black people and there's niggas. The niggas have got to go.

    Chris Rock, *Bring the Pain*, HBO, 1996

If a kid calls his grandma 'Mommy' and his mama 'Pam', he's going to jail!

    Chris Rock, *Bigger and Blacker*, HBO, 1999

Black people yelling 'racism!' White people yelling 'reverse racism!' Chinese people yelling 'sideways racism!' And the Indians ain't yelling shit, 'cause they dead. So everybody bitching about how bad their people got it: *nobody* got it worse than the American Indian. Everyone needs to calm the fuck down.

    Chris Rock, *Bigger and Blacker*, HBO, 1999

Being a star has made it possible for me to get insulted in places where the average Negro could never hope to go and get insulted.

    Sammy Davis Jr, *Yes I Can*, 1985

Beware of Greeks bearing gifts, colored men looking for loans and whites who understand the Negro.

    Adam Clayton Powell, 1908–72, black Congressman

I was so excited when I came North and sat in the front of the bus that I missed my stop.

    Dick Gregory, 1957

Some people say all black people look alike. We call those people, 'police'.

    Dave Chappelle, black comedian and screenwriter

Presidential candidate Rick Santorum is under fire for a remark he made in Iowa about black people. The remark has sparked outrage among Iowa's black community, otherwise known as Steve.

    Conan O'Brien, late-night talk-show host, 2012

What 'multiculturalism' boils down to is that you can praise any culture in the world except Western culture – and you cannot blame any culture in the world except Western culture.

Thomas Sowell, American economist and political
philosopher

#RADICALISM

No influence so quickly converts a radical into a reactionary as does his election to power.

Elizabeth Marbury, 1856–1933, American theatrical agent
and producer

The radical of one century is the conservative of the next.

Mark Twain

What this country needs is radicals who will stay that way regardless of the creeping years.

John Fischer, American writer

I never dared be radical when young, for fear it would make me conservative when old.

Robert Frost, 1874–1963, American poet, 'Precaution', 1936

It is well known that the most radical revolutionary will become a conservative the day after the revolution.

Hannah Arendt, 1906–75, German-American political
philosopher

See also: MARXISM, REVOLUTION

#REAGAN, RONALD, 1911–2004, 40TH PRESIDENT OF THE UNITED STATES, 1981–89

This fellow they've nominated claims he's the new Thomas Jefferson. Well, let me tell you something. I knew Thomas Jefferson. He was a friend of mine. And governor, you're no Thomas Jefferson.

  Ronald Reagan, answering claims by Bill Clinton's campaign, at the 1992 Republican National Convention, poking fun at his own age (See Senator Bentsen quote, p. 171)

... the acting President of the United States.

  Gore Vidal, 1925–2012, American novelist and commentator

... a triumph of the embalmer's art.

  Gore Vidal

I was cooking breakfast this morning for my kids and I thought, 'He's just like a Teflon frying pan. Nothing sticks to him.'

  Michael Kenney, *Boston Globe*, 1984

I never drink coffee at lunch – I find it keeps me awake for the afternoon.

  Ronald Reagan

I have orders to be awakened at any time in case of a national emergency, even if I'm in a Cabinet meeting.

  Ronald Reagan

I still think Nancy does most of his talking; you'll notice that she *never* drinks water when Ronnie speaks.

  Robin Williams, comedian and actor, interview in *Playboy*, 1982

But there are advantages to being elected President. The day after I was elected, I had my high school grades classified Top Secret.
  Ronald Reagan

I am not worried about the deficit. It is big enough to take care of itself.
  Ronald Reagan

I believe that Ronald Reagan can make this country what it once was – an Arctic region covered in ice.
  Steve Martin, American actor and comedian

The youthful sparkle in his eyes is caused by contact lenses, which he keeps highly polished.
  Sheilah Graham, 1904–1988, American gossip columnist

I hope you're all Republicans.
  Ronald Reagan, speaking to surgeons as he entered the
  operating room following the 1981 assassination attempt

There's a lot to be said for being nouveau riche and the Reagans mean to say it all.
  Gore Vidal

Since I came to the White House I got two hearing aids, a colon operation, skin cancer, a prostate operation and I was shot. The damn thing is, I've never felt better in my life.
  Ronald Reagan, speech to the Washington Gridiron
  Club, 1987

Ronald Reagan must love poor people because he's creating so many more of them.
    Edward Kennedy, 1932–2009, Democratic politician

The battle for the mind of Ronald Reagan was like the trench warfare of World War I. Never have so many fought so hard for such barren terrain.
    Peggy Noonan, *What I Saw at the Revolution*, 1990

Reaganomics, that makes sense to me. It means if you don't have enough money, it's because poor people are hoarding it.
    Kevin Rooney, American comedian, quoted in *GQ*, 1984

... Ronald Reagan, the President who never told bad news to the American people.
    Garrison Keillor, *We Are Still Married: Stories and Letters*,
    1989

It was the result of many years spent as a mediocre showbiz figure listening to rich, crotchety Republicans yearning for a return to the good old days.
    Mike Royko, on the roots of Reaganomics, *Chicago Tribune*

He's slightly to the right of the Sheriff of Nottingham.
    Johnny Carson, 1925–2005, late-night TV host

They say hard work never hurt anyone, but I figure why take the chance?
    Ronald Reagan

Nothing beats Reaganomics. Though herpes runs it close.
    Art Buchwald, 1925–2007, American humorous commentator

Thomas Jefferson once said, 'We should never judge a President by his age, only by his works.' And ever since he told me that, I stopped worrying.
Ronald Reagan

I want you to know that also I will not make age an issue of this campaign. I am not going to exploit, for political purposes, my opponent's youth and inexperience.
Ronald Reagan, during the 1984 Presidential debates with Walter Mondale

See also: PRESIDENCY, REPUBLICAN PARTY, WHITE HOUSE

#RELIGION

'I am all for a religious cry,' said Taper. 'It means nothing and, if successful, does not interfere with business when we are in.'
Benjamin Disraeli, 1804–81, *Coningsby*, 1844

I don't go to church much any more. I'm a Seventh-Day Absentist.
Sally Poplin

I do benefits for all religions. I'd hate to blow the hereafter on a technicality.
Bob Hope, 1903–2003, American comedian

All religions are the same, basically guilt with different holidays.
Cathy Ladman

Every day people are straying away from the church and
going back to God.
    Lenny Bruce, 1925–1966, *The Essential Lenny Bruce*, 1972

When the missionaries came to Africa, they had the Bible
and we had the land. They said, 'Let us pray.' We closed our
eyes. When we opened them, we had the Bible and they had
the land.
    Archbishop Desmond Tutu, South African priest and politician

Just going to church doesn't make you a Christian any more
than standing in your garage makes you a car.
    G. K. Chesterton, 1874–1936, English author, journalist
    and poet

Debbie: Mrs. Bartlet [the President's wife], I can't tell you
how hard I prayed for you.
Abbey: I appreciate that.
Debbie: Well, you shouldn't. I'm not very religious. So
there's the risk that my praying could be taken as insincere
or even an affront, which, if it's a vengeful God, could have
made matters worse.
Abbey: Well, it didn't, so maybe there's a clue.
    Carol Flint, *The West Wing*, 2003

People who want to share their religious views with you
almost never want you to share yours with them.
    Dave Barry, *Miami Herald*

Father Cavanaugh: You know, you remind me of the man
that lived by the river. He heard a radio report that the river
was going to rush up and flood the town. And that all the
residents should evacuate their homes. But the man said,
'I'm religious. I pray. God loves me. God will save me.'

The waters rose up. A guy in a row boat came along and he shouted, 'Hey, hey you! You in there. The town is flooding. Let me take you to safety.' But the man shouted back, 'I'm religious. I pray. God loves me. God will save me.'

A helicopter was hovering overhead. And a guy with a megaphone shouted, 'Hey you, you down there. The town is flooding. Let me drop this ladder and I'll take you to safety.' But the man shouted back that he was religious, that he prayed, that God loved him and that God will take him to safety.

Well... the man drowned. And standing at the gates of St Peter, he demanded an audience with God. 'Lord,' he said, 'I'm a religious man, I pray. I thought you loved me. Why did this happen?' God said, 'I sent you a radio report, a helicopter, and a guy in a rowboat. What the hell are you doing here?'

Aaron Sorkin, *The West Wing*, 2000

#REPUBLICAN PARTY, THE

The Republican Convention opened with a prayer. If the Lord can see his way to bless the Republican Party the way it's been carrying on, then the rest of us ought to get it without even asking.

Will Rogers, 1879–1935, American commentator and humorist, 1928

The party of Lincoln and Liberty was transmogrified into the party of hairy-backed swamp developers and corporate shills, faith-based economists, fundamentalist bullies with Bibles, Christians of convenience, freelance racists, misanthropic frat boys, shrieking midgets of AM radio, tax cheats, nihilists in golf pants, brownshirts in pinstripes, sweatshop

tycoons ... Republicans: The No. 1 reason the rest of the world thinks we're deaf, dumb and dangerous.
　Garrison Keillor, American humorist

The trouble with the Republican Party is that it has not had a new idea for thirty years.
　Woodrow Wilson, 1856–1924, 28th President of the United States, 1913–21, Democrat

They say that there's a struggle to find the soul of the Republican Party. What are they using? Tweezers and an electron microscope?
　Barry Crimmins, radio comedian

See also: REPUBLICANS, REPUBLICAN SLOGANS, TEA PARTY

#REPUBLICAN SLOGANS

If guns kill people, then spoons make Michael Moore fat.
　www.fightliberals.com

IF IGNORANCE IS BLISS, THEN YOU MUST BE ONE HAPPY LIBERAL!
　Bumper sticker, Iowa, 2010

See also: REPUBLICAN PARTY, REPUBLICANS

#REPUBLICANS

I'D VOTE FOR A REPUBLICAN
BUT I'M ALLERGIC TO NUTS!
 Bumper sticker

I like a lot of Republicans ... Indeed there are some I would trust with anything – anything, that is, except public office.
 Adlai Stevenson, 1900–1965, Governor of Illinois,
 Democratic Presidential Candidate 1952 and 1956, *New York Times*, 1953

How did sex come to be thought of as dirty in the first place? God must have been a Republican.
 Will Durst, American comedian

He's racist, he's homophobic, he's xenophobic and he's a sexist. He's the perfect Republican candidate.
 Bill Press, talk-radio host and political commentator, of Pat Buchanan, American conservative commentator

The Republicans have a habit of having three bad years and one good one and the good one always happens to be election year.
 Will Rogers

I've left specific instructions that I do not want to be brought back during a Republican administration.
 Timothy Leary, 1920–96, American psychologist and writer and enthusiast for reincarnation

A conservative Republican is one who doesn't believe anything new should ever be tried for the first time. A liberal Republican is one who *does* believe something should be tried for the first time – but not now.

Mort Sahl, American comedian

Why do Republicans fear debate? For the same reason baloney fears the slicer.

Lloyd Bentsen, 1921–2006, US Congressman and Senator, quoted on *The McLaughlin Group*, NBC TV, 1988

Lincoln was right about not fooling all the people all of the time. But the Republicans haven't given up trying.

Lyndon B. Johnson, 1908–73, 36th President of the United States, 1963–69, in 1966

See also: DEMOCRATS V. REPUBLICANS, REPUBLICAN SLOGANS, REPUBLICAN PARTY, TEA PARTY,

#REPUBLICANS V. DEMOCRATS

See DEMOCRATS V. REPUBLICANS

#REVOLUTION

Revolution: In politics, an abrupt change in the form of misgovernment.

Ambrose Bierce, 1842–1913, *The Devil's Dictionary*, 1911

A crank is a little thing that makes revolutions.

Henry George, 1839–97, US political economist

Revolution is just like one cocktail – it gets you organised for the rest.
   Will Rogers

When in doubt, burn. Fire is the revolutionary's god. Fire is instant theatre. No words can match fire.
   Jerry Rubin, 1938–94, American social activist, 1976

HAVE PATIENCE RADICALS! ROME WASN'T BURNT IN A DAY!
   Bumper sticker, Berkeley, 1969

The purity of a revolution can last a fortnight.
   Jean Cocteau, 1889–1953, French poet, novelist, dramatist and artist

Every successful revolution puts on in time the robes of the tyrant it has deposed.
   Barbara Tuchman, 1912–89, American historian and author

How a minority
Reaching majority
Seizing authority
Hates a minority.
   Leonard H. Robbins, American author, 1968

Oppressed people are frequently very oppressive when first liberated ... They know best two positions. Somebody's foot on their neck or their foot on somebody's neck.
   Florynce Kennedy, 1916–2000, American lawyer, feminist and civil rights activist

The successful revolutionary is a statesman, the unsuccessful one a criminal.
  Erich Fromm, 1900–80, American psychoanalyst and
  philosopher

Every revolution evaporates and only leaves behind the slime of a new bureaucracy.
  Franz Kafka, 1883–1924, author

See also: MARXISM, PROTEST, RADICALISM

#RICH AND POOR

We can safely abandon the doctrine of the '80s, namely that the rich were not working because they had too little money, the poor because they had too much.
  John Kenneth Galbraith, 1908–2006, Canadian-American
  economist

See also: BANKS AND BANKING, BIG BUSINESS, BUSINESS, CAPITALISM, CREDIT CRUNCH, ECONOMICS AND ECONOMISTS, ECONOMY, INFLATION, MONEY, POVERTY, STOCK MARKET AND WALL STREET, TAXATION, WEALTH

#RIGHTS

There is only one basic human right, the right to do as you damn well please. And with it comes the only basic human duty, the duty to take the consequences.
  P. J. O'Rourke, *The Liberty Manifesto*, 1993

We have the Bill of Rights. What we need is a Bill of Responsibilities.

Bill Maher, late-night talk-show host

#ROMNEY, MITT, REPUBLICAN CANDIDATE FOR 2012 PRESIDENTIAL ELECTION

Mitt Romney is quite a guy. At one point he and his wife bought a zoo and fired all the animals.

David Letterman, late-night talk-show host, 2012

During a debate, Mitt Romney said he grew up in the real streets of America. Yes, the real streets, where people pull up next to you and ask if you have any Grey Poupon.

Jimmy Kimmel, late-night talk-show host, 2012

Mitt Romney is so boring, he introduced his own fragrance called 'Unscented'.

David Letterman, 2011

Mitt Romney went to a McDonald's and ordered burgers and fries and apparently everything was going well until Romney asked the cashier if she could break a $1 million bill.

Conan O'Brien, 2012

Romney proves with a little hard work and a little luck, even a multimillionaire white guy from Harvard can succeed in this country.

Jay Leno, late-night talk-show host, 2012

I saw the young man over there with eggs Benedict, with hollandaise sauce. And I was going to suggest to you that you serve your eggs with hollandaise sauce in hubcaps. Because there's no plates like chrome for the hollandaise.

Mitt Romney, campaigning in a New Hampshire
restaurant, 2011

I love this state. The trees are the right height.

Mitt Romney, campaigning in Michigan, 2012

It's great to be here this evening in the vast, magnificent Hilton ballroom – or what Mitt Romney would call a little fixer-upper.

Barack Obama, White House Correspondents' Dinner, 2012

#ROOSEVELT, FRANKLIN D., 1882-1945, 32ND PRESIDENT OF THE UNITED STATES, 1933-45

If he became convinced tomorrow that coming out for cannibalism would get him the votes he so sorely needs, he would begin fattening a missionary in the White House backyard come Wednesday.

H. L. Mencken, 1880–1956, American essayist and critic

Meeting Franklin Roosevelt was like opening the finest bottle of champagne; knowing him was like drinking it.

Winston Churchill, 1874–1965, British statesman, orator
and writer

He had every quality that morons esteem in their heroes.

H. L. Mencken

See also: PRESIDENCY

#ROOSEVELT, THEODORE, 1858–1919, 26TH PRESIDENT OF THE UNITED STATES, 1901–09

I am only an average man, but, by George, I work at it harder than the average man.
   Theodore Roosevelt

His idea of getting hold of the right end of the stick is to snatch it from the hands of somebody who is using it effectively and to hit him over the head with it.
   George Bernard Shaw, 1856–1950, Irish playwright

I am told that he no sooner thinks than he talks, which is a miracle not wholly in accord with an educational theory of forming an opinion.
   Woodrow Wilson

One always thinks of him as a glorified bouncer engaged eternally in cleaning out bar-rooms – and not too proud to gouge when the inspiration came to him, or to bite in the clinches.
   H. L. Mencken, *Prejudices*, Second Series, 1920

The great virtue of my radicalism lies in the fact that I am perfectly ready, if necessary, to be radical on the conservative side.
   Theodore Roosevelt, 1906

Whenever you are asked if you can do a job, tell 'em, 'Certainly, I can!' Then get busy and find out how to do it.
   Theodore Roosevelt

See also: PRESIDENCY

#ROYALTY

The first king was a fortunate soldier.
    Voltaire, 1694–1778, French writer, historian and philosopher

After you've met more than 150 Lord Mayors, they all begin to look the same.
    King George V, 1865–1936 (attrib.)

If this is the way Queen Victoria treats her convicts, she doesn't deserve to have any.
    Oscar Wilde, 1854–1900, Irish playwright, imprisoned in Reading Gaol

In a few years there will be only five kings in the world; the King of England and the four kings in a pack of cards.
    King Farouk of Egypt, 1920–65, in 1953

When the king is said to be a good fellow, his reign is a failure.
    Napoleon Bonaparte, 1769–1821, French military and political leader and Emperor

... all kings is mostly rapscallions ...
    Mark Twain, *The Adventures of Huckleberry Finn*, 1884

It has been said, not truly but within a possible approximation of truth, that in 1802 every hereditary monarch was insane.
    Walter Bagehot, 1826–77, English essayist, journalist and businessman

I think it's a perfectly valid system for producing a head of state. It's been very successful for a thousand years. It's had its ups and downs, undoubtedly.
    Prince Philip, the Duke of Edinburgh, on the monarchy

S

#SCIENCE

Our scientific power has outrun our spiritual power. We have guided missiles and misguided men.
   Martin Luther King Jr, 1929–68, American clergyman, activist and civil rights leader

We need science to help us solve all the problems we wouldn't have if there were no science.
   Sally Poplin, English humorous writer

Science is always wrong. It never solves a problem without creating ten more.
   George Bernard Shaw, 1856–1950, Irish playwright

Scientists – the crowd that for dash and style make the general public look like the Bloomsbury set.
   Fran Lebowitz, New York humorist

Sam: I need you to tell me everything you can tell me about the superconducting supercollider.
Professor Milgate: How much time do we have?
Sam: About ten minutes.
Professor Milgate: If you pay very close attention, stay very, very quiet – I can teach you how to spell it.
   Aaron Sorkin, *The West Wing*, 2002

#SCOTLAND AND THE SCOTS

It is never difficult to distinguish between a Scotsman with a grievance and a ray of sunshine.
   P. G. Wodehouse, 1881–1975, *Blandings Castle and Elsewhere*, 1935

There are few more impressive sights in the world than a Scotsman on the make.
   J. M. Barrie, 1860–1937, *What Every Woman Knows*, 1908

The noblest prospect that the Scotchman ever sees is the high road that leads him to England.
   Samuel Johnson, 1709–84, English poet, essayist and lexicographer

Q: Why do people write 'F*** the Pope' on walls?
A: It takes too long to write 'F*** the Moderator of the United Reformed Church of Scotland'.
   Anon.

Scotland, land of the omnipotent No.
   Alan Bold, 1943–98, *A Memory of Death*, 1969

Cameron offers Scotland the 'haggis' agreement. No one will ever be quite sure what's in it.
   Alan Mills, tweet, February 2012

See also: BRITAIN AND THE BRITISH

#SLOGANS

I have what it takes to take what you've got!
James H. Boren, 1925–2010, humorist and academic, when
running for President

YEAH, WELL, YOU KNOW, THAT'S JUST LIKE, UH, YOUR
OPINION, MAN.
All-purpose protest sign, Washington 2010

GENERIC ANGRY SLOGAN!
All-purpose protest sign, America

WHAT DO WE WANT?!
RESPECTFUL DISCOURSE
WHEN DO WE WANT IT?!
NOW WOULD BE AGREEABLE TO ME, BUT I AM INTERESTED
IN YOUR OPINION.
Sign at protest, Washington, 2010

And take it off CAPS LOCK
Protest march, Washington

PROTEST SIGNS ARE AN INEFFECTUAL WAY OF COMMUNICAT-
ING NUANCED VIEWS ON ISSUES THAT CANNOT + SHOULD
NOT BE REDUCED TO SIMPLE PITHY SLOGANS
Sign, march, Washington, 2010

Gay Whales Against the Bomb
1980s satirical slogan

Help Stamp Out Footprints!
Anon.

What do we want?
Gradual change!
When do we want it?
In due course!
  Manifesto of the All-in-Good-Time Conservative Party

See also: DEMOCRAT SLOGANS, PROTEST,
REPUBLICAN SLOGANS, TEA PARTY

#SOCIAL MEDIA

EVERY POTENTIAL 2040 PRESIDENT ALREADY UNELECTABLE
DUE TO FACEBOOK
  NATION FACING LEADERSHIP VACUUM IN 2040
  MAJORITY OF RHODES SCHOLARS PICTURED DOING
KEG STANDS
  MOST WOMEN HAVE POLITICAL-CAREER-ENDING SEXY
HALLOWEEN PICTURES
  Onion News Network, 2012

Privacy is dead, and social media hold the smoking gun.
  Pete Cashmore, CEO, Mashable, 2011

Don't say anything online that you wouldn't want plastered
on a billboard with your face on it.
  Erin Bury, Sprouter community manager, 2010

You are what you tweet.
  Sally Poplin

Too many tweets make a twat.
  David Cameron, Conservative Prime Minister, 2009

The Republican Presidential candidates held a debate on Twitter. It combined the excitement of C-SPAN with the suspense of typing.

Jimmy Kimmel, late-night talk-show host, 2011

Now more than ever it's clear that media is changing. New outlets are adapting to an online world. Even Bloomberg News is on Twitter, with an impressive 220,000 followers; so only 20,000 less than a cobra that escaped from the Bronx zoo.

Seth Meyers, White House Correspondents' Dinner, 2011

What do we want? Italics in tweets! When do we want them? *Now*

Matt Leys, tweet, 2012

You can tell why the Grand Old Duke of York had 10,000 followers. Classic tweets like 'Going up a hill! lol' and 'OMG Going down a hill!'

sarcasticapple, tweet, 2012

See also: INTERNET

#SOCIALISM

The problem with socialism is that you eventually run out of other people's money.

Margaret Thatcher, Conservative Prime Minister 1979–90 (attrib.)

What Socialists are always aiming at is a paternal government under which they are to be the spoilt children.

Sir Arthur Helps, 1813–1875, *Thoughts on Government*, 1872

He had a peculiar vague horror of Socialism, which he regarded as a compound of atheism, republicanism, blight, mildew, measles and all the worst characteristics of the Continental sabbath.

H. G. Wells, 1866–1946, *Bealby*, 1915

To grasp the true meaning of socialism, imagine a world where everything is designed by the post office, even the sleaze.

P. J. O'Rourke, libertarian journalist and commentator

Socialism is, among other things, the political habitat of low self-esteem, incompetence, self-loathing, and a willingness to steal – or have stolen for you – what you are unable or unwilling to work for. Socialism is a philosophy fit only for slugs, leeches and mosquitoes.

L. Neil Smith, libertarian author, *Alice Shrugged*, 2008

Socialists make the mistake of confusing individual worth with success. They believe you cannot allow people to succeed in case those who fail feel worthless.

Kenneth Baker, Conservative Cabinet minister

Socialism only works in two places: Heaven, where they don't need it, and Hell, where they already have it.

Ronald Reagan, 1911–2004, 40th President of the United States, 1981–89

Socialism in general has a record of failure so blatant that only an intellectual could ignore or evade it.

Thomas Sowell, American economist and political philosopher

We'll find it very difficult to explain to the voters that simply by taking over Marks & Spencer we can make it as efficient as the Co-op.

Harold Wilson, 1916–95, Labour Prime Minister, 1964–70, 1974–76, in 1973

The typical Socialist ... a prim little man with a white-collar job, usually a secret teetotaller and often with vegetarian leanings ... with a social position he has no intention of forfeiting.

George Orwell, 1903–1950, *The Road to Wigan Pier*, 1937

Once the government has embarked upon a course of making all things fair, where is it to stop? Will tall people have to walk around on their knees? Will fat people be strapped to helium balloons? Will attractive people be made to wear ridiculous haircuts?

P. J. O'Rourke, *The Enemies List*, 1996

If Socialism means anything, surely, it means the state confiscating whatever you have that other people don't.

Oliver Metcalf, political philosopher

I love it when people dress up their desire to have things without paying for them as some sort of noble progressive cause.

Ben Goldacre, science writer

Socialism is a philosophy of failure, the creed of ignorance, and the gospel of envy, its inherent virtue is the equal sharing of misery.

Winston Churchill, 1874–1965, British statesman, orator and writer

Socialism in Eight Words:

Pacifying your own conscience with other people's money.
  Rob Summerfield, tweet

Starvation? Who cares. At least nobody is rich.
  Thomas Dalton, tweet

Subcontracting compassion to feckless bureaucrats and greedy politicians.
  Jon G., tweet

Making everyone equally ignorant, poor, depressed and miserable.
  Resist Tyranny, tweet

It's never worked before, but let's try again.
  Oliver Cooper, tweet
  #socialismineightwords, Twitter, December 2011

Socialism has been tried many, many times. It has failed every single time.
  It does not work and indeed cannot work because, simply, humans are not the way it requires them to be.
  Euangray, Comment is Free, 2011

As far as Socialism means anything, it must be about the wider distribution of smoked salmon and caviar.
  Sir Richard Marsh, 1928–2011, former Labour Cabinet
  Minister, quoted in *The Observer*, 1976

As with the Christian religion, the worst advertisement for Socialism is its adherents.
  George Orwell, *The Road to Wigan Pier*, 1937

At one time Socialism might have been a good idea. Its inspiration, in those days, was generous and humane. Nowadays, it can appeal only to those whose social maladjustment might otherwise push them into the criminal classes, or whose intellectual inadequacies make them hungry for a dogmatic system in which they can hide their inability to think for themselves.

Auberon Waugh, 1939–2001, novelist and journalist, *The Spectator*, 1984

We should have had socialism already but for the socialists.

George Bernard Shaw

An inevitable consequence of socialism is the division of society into two groups: those who are consuming government 'services' and those who are paying for them.

Lee Robinson, American author

... Fabled names in the annals of the New Left. All with monosyllabic names ... Stan, Mike, Les, Norm. As if to have two syllables in one's name were an indication of social pretension.

Alan Bennett, *Getting On*, 1971

The function of socialism is to raise suffering to a higher level.

Norman Mailer, 1923–2007, American novelist

'Rabbi, can one build socialism in one country?'
'Yes, my son, but one must live in another.'

Anon., quoted in *The Spectator*, 1984

Socialists cry 'Power to the people', and raise the clenched fist as they say it. We all know what they really mean – power over people, power to the State.

Margaret Thatcher, speech, 1986

See also: COMMUNISM, CUBA, EQUALITY, FASCISM, LABOUR PARTY, THE LEFT, LEFT V. RIGHT, MARXISM, NORTH KOREA, SOCIALISM V. CAPITALISM

#SOCIALISM V. CAPITALISM

The inherent vice of capitalism is the unequal sharing of blessings; the inherent vice of socialism is the equal sharing of miseries.

Winston Churchill, speech in the House of Commons, 1945

Socialism is when the state owns everything; capitalism is when your bank does.

Anon.

Capitalism works better than it sounds, while socialism sounds better than it works.

Richard Nixon, 1913–94, 37th President of the United States, 1969–74

Capitalism and communism stand at opposite poles. Their essential difference is this: The communist, seeing the rich man and his fine home, says: 'No man should have so much.' The capitalist, seeing the same thing, says: 'All men should have as much.'

Phelps Adams, American writer and executive

See also: CAPITALISM, COMMUNISM, FASCISM,
LABOUR PARTY, LEFT, LEFT V. RIGHT, MARXISM,
SOCIALISM

#SPEAKERS AND SPEECHES

Nothing is so unbelievable that oratory cannot make it
acceptable.
> Cicero, 106–43 BC, Roman philosopher, orator and
> political theorist

If I am to speak for ten minutes, I need a week for preparation; if fifteen minutes, three days; if half an hour, two days;
if an hour, I am ready now.
> Woodrow Wilson, 1856–1924, 28th President of the United
> States, 1913–21

I think this is the most extraordinary collection of talent,
of human knowledge, that has ever been gathered at the
White House – with the possible exception of when Thomas
Jefferson dined alone.
> John F. Kennedy, 1917–63, 35th President of the United
> States, 1961–63, address at a White House dinner honour-
> ing Nobel Prize winners, 1962

If you can't convince them, confuse them.
> Harry S. Truman, 1884–1972, 33rd President of the United
> States, 1945–53

Oratory is the power to talk people out of their sober and
natural opinions.
> Paul Chatfield, 1779–1849, English poet and humorist

If half the people who make speeches would make concrete floors instead, they would be doing more good.
  Lord Darling, 1849–1936, English lawyer, politician and
  High Court judge

I sometimes marvel at the extraordinary docility with which Americans submit to speeches.
  Adlai Stevenson, 1900–1965, Governor of Illinois,
  Democratic Presidential Candidate 1952 and 1956

Making a speech on economics is a bit like pissing down your leg. It seems hot to you but never to anyone else.
  Lyndon B. Johnson, 1908–73, 36th President of the United
  States, 1963–69

Why don't th' feller who says, 'I'm not a speechmaker,' let it go at that instead o' givin' a demonstration?
  Kin Hubbard, 1868–1930, American cartoonist, humorist
  and journalist

A graduation ceremony is an event where the commencement speaker tells thousands of students dressed in identical caps and gowns that 'individuality' is the key to success.
  Robert Purvis, 1810–98, African-American activist

When politicians call for 'quiet reflection', you know something has happened for which they didn't have a speech ready.
  Andrew Marr, BBC political interviewer

I can still remember the first time I ever heard Hubert Humphrey speak. He was in the second hour of a five-minute talk.
  Gerald Ford, 1913–2006, 38th President of the United States,
  1974–77, of the US Vice President under Lyndon B. Johnson

An after-dinner speech should be like a lady's dress:
long enough to cover the subject and short enough to
be interesting.

    Anon.

The best audience is intelligent, well-educated and a little
drunk.

    Alben W. Barkley, 1877–1956, Vice President under Harry
    S. Truman, 1949–53

I stand up when he nudges me. I sit down when they pull
my coat.

    Ernest Bevin, 1881–1951, British trades union leader and
    Labour politician

Hubert Humphrey talks so fast that listening to him is like
trying to read *Playboy* magazine with your wife turning
over the pages.

    Barry Goldwater, 1909–98, United States Senator from
    Arizona

This is a moment I deeply wish my parents could have
lived to share. My father would have enjoyed what you
have so generously said of me – and my mother would have
believed it.

    Lyndon B. Johnson, responding to an introduction before
    the dedication of Summersville reservoir, West Virginia,
    1966

It usually takes me more than three weeks to prepare a
good impromptu speech.

    Mark Twain, 1835–1910, American writer and humorist

I like the way you always manage to state the obvious with a sense of real discovery.

   Gore Vidal, 1925–2012, *The Best Man*, 1960

It just shows, what any Member of Parliament will tell you, that if you want real oratory, the preliminary noggin is essential. Unless pie-eyed, you cannot hope to grip.

   P. G. Wodehouse, *Right Ho, Jeeves*, 1934

The whole art of a political speech is to put *nothing* into it. It is much more difficult than it sounds.

   Hilaire Belloc, 1870–1953, *A Conversation with an Angel and Other Essays*, 1928

Hubert, a speech does not need to be eternal to be immortal.

   Muriel Humphrey, 1912–98, wife Hubert Humphrey

You spoke so flatteringly about me that for a moment I thought I was dead.

   Harry S. Truman, reacting to praise from Israeli ambassador Abba Eban

Chairman: Chauncey Depew can always produce a speech. All you have to do is give him his dinner and up comes his speech.
Chauncey Depew: I only hope that it isn't true that if I give you my speech, up will come your dinner.

   Chauncey Depew, 1834–1928, nineteenth-century railroad executive and US Senator

The best way to stay awake during an after-dinner speech is to give it.

   Sally Poplin

The politicians were talking themselves red, white and blue in the face.

> Clare Boothe Luce, 1903–87, American playwright, editor, ambassador and Congresswoman

My father gave me these hints on speechmaking: 'Be sincere, be brief ... be seated.'

> James Roosevelt, 1907–91, oldest son of Franklin D. Roosevelt and United States Congressman

There are three golden rules for parliamentary speakers: stand up, speak up and shut up.

> James Lowther, 1855–1949, Conservative politician and Speaker of the House of Commons, 1905–21

A good speech may not always be remembered but a bad speech is never forgotten – or forgiven.

> Bernard Weatherill, 1920–2007, Conservative politician and Speaker of the House of Commons, 1983–92

The compulsion of politicians to talk too much is in our day a very big obstacle to accomplishing what they all say they want to do.

> Walter Lippmann, 1889–1974, American intellectual, writer and political commentator

According to most studies, people's number one fear is public speaking. Death is number two. Does that seem right? That means to the average person, if you have to go to a funeral, you're better off in the casket than doing the eulogy.

> Jerry Seinfeld, actor and stand-up comedian

The great orator always shows a dash of contempt for the opinions of his audience.
   Elbert Hubbard, 1856–1915, American publisher, artist, essayist and poet

I do not object to people looking at their watches when I am speaking – but I strongly object when they start shaking them to make certain they are still going.
   Lord Birkett, 1883–1962, MP and lawyer, 1960 (attrib.)

Desperately accustomed as I am to public speaking.
   Noël Coward, 1899–1973, English actor and writer, opening charity bazaar at Oxford (attrib.)

He can take a batch of words and scramble them together and leaven them properly with a hunk of oratory and knock the White House doorknob right out of a candidate's hand.
   Will Rogers, 1879–1935, American commentator and humorist, on William Jennings Bryan, Democrat who stood three times for President. Contesting the 1896 election, he made 500 speeches in a year

He is one of those orators of whom it was well said, 'Before they get up, they do not know what they are going to say; when they are speaking, they do not know what they are saying; and when they have sat down, they do not know what they have said.'
   Winston Churchill, speech, House of Commons, 1912

Better keep your mouth shut and be thought a fool than open it and remove all doubt.
   Attributed to Abraham Lincoln, Mark Twain, Oscar Wilde, Denis Thatcher and many others

A speech is like a love affair. Any fool can start it but to end it requires considerable skill .
  Lord Mancroft, 1914–87, Conservative peer

The human brain starts working the moment you are born and never stops until you stand up to speak in public.
  Sir George Jessel, 1824–1883, English industrialist and
  Justice of the Peace

I am the most spontaneous speaker in the world because every word, every gesture, and every retort has been carefully rehearsed.
  George Bernard Shaw

The last time I was in this hall was when my late beloved boss, Frank Knox, the Secretary of the Navy, spoke here, and it was a better speech he gave than the one I'll be giving tonight. I know. I wrote them both.
  Adlai Stevenson

Humming, Hawing and Hesitation are the three Graces of contemporary Parliamentary oratory.
  Julian Critchley, 1930–2000, Conservative MP,
  Westminster Blues, 1985

Consummate use of epiplexis, tricolon thrown in with epistrophe encompassed in an act of pathos rarely seen convincingly delivered by a political speaker. It worked.
  Mario Creatura, analysing Boris Johnson's eve-of-Olympics
  rallying cry, Platform 10 blog, 27 July 2012

Toby: You want the benefits of free trade? Food is cheaper.

Policewoman: Yes.

Toby: Food is cheaper! Clothes are cheaper, steel is cheaper, cars are cheaper ... Phone service is cheaper! You feel me building a rhythm here? That's because I'm a speech writer and I know how to make a point.

Policewoman: Toby.

Toby: It lowers prices, and it raises income. You see what I did with 'lowers' and 'raises' there? It's called the science of listener attention. We did repetition, we did floating opposites, and now you end with the one that's not like the others. Ready? Free trade stops wars. And that's it. Free trade stops wars, and we figure out how to fix the rest. One world, one peace... I'm sure I've seen that on a sign somewhere.

   Paul Redford and Aaron Sorkin, *The West Wing*, 2001

Toby: Call and response isn't going to work in front of a Joint Session. You're alliteration happy: 'guardians of gridlock', 'protectors of privilege'. I needed an avalanche of Advil. And when you use pop-culture references, your speech has a shelf-life of twelve minutes. You don't mind constructive criticism, do you?

   Aaron Sorkin, *The West Wing*, 2002

#SPORT

If only Hitler and Mussolini could have a good game of bowls once a week at Geneva, I feel that Europe would not be as troubled as it is.

   R. G. Briscow, British politician, during the Second World War

One lesson you better learn if you want to be in politics, is that you never go out on a golf course and beat the President.

Lyndon B. Johnson

No country which has cricket as one of its national games has yet gone communist.

Woodrow Wyatt, 1918–97, Labour MP and columnist

There's a hell of a lot of politics in football. I don't think Henry Kissinger would have lasted forty-eight hours at Old Trafford.

Tommy Docherty, Scottish footballer and sometime
manager at Old Trafford

There are some remarkable parallels between basketball and politics. Michael Jordan has already mastered the skill needed for political success: how to stay aloft without visible means of support.

Margaret Thatcher, 1992

Internationally, football has become a substitute for war.

Jeremy Paxman, British TV interviewer and author

#STOCK MARKET AND WALL STREET

The United States has a new weapon. It destroys people but leaves buildings still standing. It's called the stock market.

Jay Leno, late-night talk-show host

Can we trust Wall Street any more?

Looks like the future of 'invest' is going to have to be 'investigation'.

Sally Poplin

When I saw how badly my shares were doing, I tried to call my broker. But his ledge was busy.

Sally Poplin

Wall Street indexes predicted nine out of the last five recessions.

Paul A. Samuelson, 1915–2009, American economist,
quoted in *Newsweek*, 1966

T

#TAXATION

Tax reform means, 'Don't tax you, don't tax me, tax that fellow behind the tree.'
  Russell Long, 1918–2003, United States Senator from Louisiana

Blessed are the young, for they shall inherit the national debt.
  Herbert Hoover, 1874–1964, 31ˢᵗ President of the United States, 1929–33

There is one difference between a tax collector and a taxidermist – the taxidermist leaves the hide.
  Mortimer Caplan, b. 1916, Commissioner of the Internal Revenue Service in the 1960s, in *Time* magazine, 1963

Perhaps the government thinks that a tax is the best form of defence.
  On hearing that the Inland Revenue has more employees than the Royal Navy, Antony Jay and Jonathan Lynn, *Yes Minister*, 1980

The rich aren't like us; they pay less taxes.
  Peter de Vries, 1910–93, American novelist

The Eiffel Tower is the Empire State Building after taxes.
   Anon.

The income tax people are very nice. They're letting me
keep my own mother.
   Henny Youngman, 1908–98, American stand-up comic

Thank goodness we don't get all of the government that we
are made to pay for.
   Milton Friedman, 1912–2006, American economist

The taxpayer – that's someone who works for the federal
government but doesn't have to take a civil service examination.
   Ronald Reagan, 1911–2004, 40th President of the United
   States, 1981–89

The Lord giveth and the tax man taketh away.
   Sally Poplin, English humorous writer

You're forgetting the basic principle of taxation – the
government knows how to spend your money better than
you do!
   Sally Poplin

I used to say I was making a speech on the Senate floor
and I said, 'Now, gentlemen, let me tax your memories,' and
Kennedy jumped up and said, 'Why haven't we thought of
that before?'
   Bob Dole, quoted in *GQ*, 1999

But in this world, nothing is certain except death and taxes.
   Benjamin Franklin, 1705–90, author, politician, satirist,
   musician, inventor and one of the Founding Fathers of the
   United States

Elections should be held on 16 April – the day after we pay our income taxes. That is one of the few things that might discourage politicians from being big spenders.
  Thomas Sowell, American economist and political philosopher

A government which robs Peter to pay Paul can always depend on the support of Paul.
  George Bernard Shaw, 1856–1950, *Everybody's Political What's What?*, 1944

I'm proud to be paying taxes in the United States. The only thing is, I could be just as proud on half the money.
  Arthur Godfrey, 1903–83, American radio and television entertainer

We'll try to cooperate fully with the IRS, because, as citizens, we feel a strong patriotic duty not to go to jail.
  Dave Barry, *Miami Herald*

Taxation: the process by which money is collected from the people to pay the salaries of the men who do the collecting.
  Anon.

The idea that a nation can tax itself into prosperity is one of the cruellest delusions which has befuddled the human mind.
  Ronald Reagan, speech 1982, wrongly attributing it to Winston Churchill

You don't pay taxes; they take taxes.
  Chris Rock, American comedian

While no one likes paying taxes, we should all remember what our taxes pay for: blowing people up.
  Craig Kilborn, late-night talk-show host

Last night in his speech, President Bush called for a complete overhaul of the tax code. He said he was shocked to find out that some millionaires in this country were still paying taxes.
    Jay Leno, late-night talk-show host

Any reasonable system of taxation should be based on the slogan of 'Soak the Rich'.
    Heywood Broun, 1888–1939, American newspaper
    columnist and editor

No nation has ever taxed itself to prosperity.
    Dick Cheney, Vice President, speech, Washington, March
    2007

Why does a slight tax increase cost you two hundred dollars and a substantial tax cut save you thirty cents?
    Peg Bracken, 1918–2007, American humorous writer

See also: GOVERNMENT, WASHINGTON

#TEA PARTY, THE

I am not the first to note the vast differences between the Wall Street protesters and the tea partiers. To name three: The tea partiers have jobs, showers and a point.
    Ann Coulter, American commentator and controversialist,
    October 2011

Socialism? Not on my watch!
    T-shirt slogan

I AM NOT YOUR ATM!
    Tea Party bumper sticker

Party like it's 1773!
  Tea Party T-shirt, Washington 2010

TEA PARTY? WHITE WHINE PARTY
IS MORE LIKE IT!
  Bumper sticker

HONK IF MY TAXES SUPPORT
YOUR WHINY TEABAGGING ASS!
  Bumper sticker

A Tea Party group is running a summer camp for kids. It's
the only camp where the kids sit around a bonfire and hear
scary stories about taxing the richest two per cent.
  Conan O'Brien, late-night talk-show host, 2011

See also: SARAH PALIN, PROTEST, REPUBLICAN
PARTY, REPUBLICANS

#TELEVISION

Television has made dictatorship impossible but democracy
unbearable.
  Shimon Peres, Israeli Prime Minister, 1995–96, 9th President
  of Israel

Television is to news what bumper stickers are to philosophy.
  Richard Nixon, 1913–94, 37th President of the United
  States, 1969–74

Time has convinced me of one thing: television is for
appearing on, not looking at.
  Noël Coward, 1899–1973, English actor and writer (attrib.)

Broadcasting is really too important to be left to the broadcasters.
   Tony Benn, Labour politician

Rush Limbaugh is OK after being released from a Hawaiian hospital after a heart scare. Fox News sent flowers; MSNBC sent cheese fries.
   Jay Leno

The idea of a news broadcast once was to find someone with information and broadcast it. The idea now is to find someone with ignorance and spread it around.
   P. J. O'Rourke, *Peace Kills: America's Fun New Imperialism*, 2004

See also: PRESS

#TERRORISM

See WAR ON TERROR

#THATCHER, MARGARET, CONSERVATIVE PRIME MINISTER, 1979–90

The nanny seemed to be extinct until 1975, when, like the coelacanth, she suddenly and unexpectedly reappeared in the shape of Margaret Thatcher.
   Simon Hoggart, *The Guardian*

Every Prime Minister needs a Willie.
   Margaret Thatcher, referring to her Deputy Prime Minister William Whitelaw, quoted in *The Economist*

To those waiting with bated breath for that favourite media catch-phrase, the U-turn, I have only this to say: you turn if you want, the lady's not for turning.

Margaret Thatcher, speech to the Conservative Party Conference, 1980, on her determination to persist in monetarist policies

If you want something said, ask a man. If you want something done, ask a woman.

Margaret Thatcher

It may be the cock that crows, but it is the hen that lays the eggs.

Margaret Thatcher

To wear your heart on your sleeve isn't a very good plan; you should wear it inside, where it functions best.

Margaret Thatcher

It's a funny old world.

Margaret Thatcher, opening remarks to the Cabinet on 22 November 1990, announcing her decision to withdraw from the Conservative leadership contest

I am extraordinarily patient, provided I get my own way in the end.

Margaret Thatcher, 1989

I cannot bring myself to vote for a woman who has been voice-trained to speak to me as though my dog had just died.

Keith Waterhouse, 1929–2009, English novelist and columnist

Standing in the middle of the road is very dangerous; you get knocked down by the traffic from both sides.
Margaret Thatcher

Paddy Ashdown is the only party leader who's a trained killer. Although, to be fair, Mrs Thatcher was self-taught.
Charles Kennedy, Liberal Democrat party leader 1999–2006

... Pétain in petticoats.
Denis Healey, Labour Chancellor of the Exchequer, 1974–79

... a bargain basement Boudicca.
Denis Healey

To quote her own backbenchers, the Great She-Elephant, She-Who-Must-Be-Obeyed, the Catherine the Great of Finchley, the Prime Minister herself.
Denis Healey, speech in the House of Commons, 1984

Margaret Thatcher adds the diplomacy of Alf Garnett to the economics of Arthur Daley.
Denis Healey

She was a tigress surrounded by hamsters.
John Biffen, 1930–2007, Conservative politician, *The Observer*, 1990

She has Marilyn Monroe's mouth and Caligula's eyes.
François Mitterand, 1916–96, 21st President of France

I am not prepared to accept the economics of a housewife.
Jacques Chirac, French Prime Minister and President, 1995–2007, quoted in the *Sunday Times*, 1987

Like the bubonic plague and stone cladding, no one took Margaret Thatcher seriously until it was too late.
Anon.

She is the Enid Blyton of economics. Nothing must be allowed to spoil her simple plots.
Richard Holme, 1936–2008, Liberal bigwig, 1980

Don't think of her as a politician. Think of her as a one-woman revolution – a hurricane in human form.
Andrew Marr, British journalist

I wear the pants in our house but I also wash and iron them.
Denis Thatcher, 1915–2003, husband (attrib.)

She cannot see an institution without hitting it with her handbag.
Julian Critchley, 1930–2000, Conservative MP, *The Times*, 1982

The further you got from Britain, the more admired you found she was.
James Callaghan, 1912–2005, Labour Prime Minister, 1976–79, *The Spectator*, 1990

Attila the Hen.
Clement Freud, 1924–2009, Liberal MP

... the parrot on Ronald Reagan's shoulder.
Denis Healey

The Prime Minister tells us she has given the French President a piece of her mind – not a gift I would receive with alacrity.
  Denis Healey

If I were married to her, I'd be sure to have dinner ready when she got home.
  George Shultz, economist, American Secretary of State
  (attrib.)

She's democratic enough to talk down to anyone.
  Austin Mitchell, Labour MP

See also: THE CONSERVATIVE PARTY, CONSERVATIVES AND CONSERVATISM

#TRADES UNIONS

Trades unions are islands of anarchy in a sea of chaos.
  Aneurin Bevan, 1897–1960, Welsh Labour politician

I'm going to my cake-decorating class. I don't really want to, but we're electing a new secretary and it's like everything else: if the rank and file don't go, the militants take over.
  Alan Bennett, *Habeas Corpus*, 1973

Unionism seldom, if ever, uses such power as it has to insure better work; almost always it devotes a large part of that power to safeguarding bad work.
  H. L. Mencken, 1880–1956, *Prejudices*, Third Series, 1922

The most conservative man in the world is the British Trade Unionist when you want to change him.

> Ernest Bevin, 1881–1951, British trades union leader and Labour politician, speech, Trades Union Congress, 1927

See also: LABOUR PARTY, SOCIALISM, WORK

#TRUMAN, HARRY S., 1884-1972, 33RD PRESIDENT OF THE UNITED STATES, 1945-53

The Buck Stops Here.

> Slogan on President Truman's desk

To err is Truman.

> Republican Party slogan, 1948 election

I never did give anybody hell. I just told the truth and they thought it was hell.

> Harry S. Truman, who, during the 1948 election campaign, earned the nickname, 'Give 'Em Hell, Harry'

Always be sincere, even if you don't mean it.

> Harry S. Truman

If I hadn't been President of the United States, I probably would have ended up a piano player in a bawdy house.

> Harry S. Truman

Harry S. Truman rules the country with an iron fist, the same way he plays the piano.

> Bob Hope, 1903–2003, American comedian

My father was not a failure. After all, he was the father of a President of the United States.
  Harry S. Truman

Well, I wouldn't say that I was in the 'great' class, but I had a great time while I was trying to be great.
  Harry S. Truman

Mr Truman believes other people should be 'free to govern themselves as they see fit' – so long as they see fit to see as we see fit.
  I. F. Stone, 1907–89, American journalist and iconoclast

See also: PRESIDENCY, WHITE HOUSE

#TRUTH

Never believe anything in politics until it has been officially denied.
  Otto von Bismarck, 1815–98, German statesman and
  Minister President of Prussia, 1862–90

It has always been desirable to tell the truth, but seldom if ever necessary to tell the whole truth.
  Arthur Balfour, 1848–1930, Conservative politician and
  Prime Minister 1902–05

Truth is a rare and precious commodity. We must be sparing in its use.
  B. P. Scott, *The Spectator*, 1982

If one tells the truth, one is sure, sooner or later, to be found out.

> Oscar Wilde, 1854–1900, *Phrases and Philosophies for the Use of the Young*, 1894

See also: LIES AND LYING

#TYLER, JOHN, 1790-1862, 10TH PRESIDENT OF THE UNITED STATES, 1841-45

John Tyler has been called a mediocre man but this is unwarranted flattery. He was a politician of monumental littleness.

> Theodore Roosevelt, 1858–1919, 26th President, 1901–09

See also: PRESIDENCY, WHITE HOUSE

#TYRANTS

Tyrants are always assassinated too late; that is their great excuse.

> E. M. Cioran, 1911–95, Romanian philosopher

So long as men worship the Caesars and Napoleons, Caesars and Napoleons will duly rise and make them miserable.

> Aldous Huxley, 1894–1963, English humanist, pacifist, poet and novelist

See also: DICTATORSHIP

V

#VICE PRESIDENCY, THE AMERICAN

The Vice Presidency of the United States isn't worth a warm pitcher of spit.

John Nance Garner, 1868–1967, 32nd Vice President of the United States, 1933–41

Worst damn fool mistake I ever made was letting myself be elected Vice President of the United States ... I spent eight long years as Mr Roosevelt's spare tyre.

John Nance Garner, quoted in *Saturday Evening Post*, 1963

The man with the best job in the country is the Vice President. All he has to do is get up every morning and say, 'How's the President?'

Will Rogers, 1879–1935, American commentator and humorist, 1934

Once there were two brothers: one ran away to sea, the other was elected Vice President – and nothing was heard from either of them again.

Thomas Marshall, 1854–1925, 28th Vice President of the United States, 1913–21

Democracy means that anyone can grow up to be President and anyone who doesn't grow up can be Vice President.
Johnny Carson, late-night talk-show host

You really do get a chance to meet dead leaders ... it's known as quiet diplomacy.
George H. W. Bush, on the number of state funerals he'd attended in four years as Vice President, speech in Washington, 1985

The Vice Presidency is sort of like the last cookie on the plate. Everybody insists he won't take it, but somebody always does.
Bill Vaughan, 1915–77, American columnist and aphorist

There is absolutely no circumstance whatever under which I would accept that spot. Even if they tied and gagged me, I would find a way to signal by wiggling my ears.
Ronald Reagan, 1911–2004, 40th President of the United States, 1981–89, on the possibility of being offered the Vice Presidency in 1968

All that Hubert needs over there is a gal to answer the phone and a pencil with an eraser on it.
Lyndon B. Johnson, 1908–73, 36th President of the United States, 1963–69, on his Vice President Hubert Humphrey

Toby: In a triumph of the middling, a nod to mediocrity, and with gorge rising, it gives me great nausea to announce Robert Russell – Bingo Bob, himself – as your new Vice President.
Will: This lapdog of the mining interests is as dull as he is unremarkable ...
Toby: ... as lacklustre as he is soporific. This reversion to the mean ...

Will: ... this rebuke to the exemplary ...
Toby: ... gives hope to the millions unfavoured by the exceptional ... Bob Russell: not the worst, not the best, just what we're stuck with.
Peter Noah, *The West Wing*, 2003

See also: JOE BIDEN, PRESIDENCY, DAN QUAYLE

#VOTING

I never vote *for* anyone. I always vote against.
W. C. Fields, 1880–1946, American comedian

If God had wanted us to vote, he would have given us candidates.
Graffito, New York, 2007

If voting changed anything, they'd abolish it.
Graffito, London, 1989

It makes no difference who you vote for. The two parties are really one party, representing 4 per cent of the people.
Gore Vidal, 1925–2012, American author, playwright and commentator

Ballots are the rightful and peaceful successors of bullets.
Abraham Lincoln, 1809–65, 16th President of the United States, 1861–65

Voting Tory will cause your wife to have bigger breasts and increase your chances of owning a BMW M3.
Boris Johnson, Conservative politician, during 2005 election

Decisions are made by those who show up.
   Anon.

President: I was watching a television program before, with a kind of roving moderator who spoke to a seated panel of young women who were having some sort of problem with their boyfriends – apparently because the boyfriends had all slept with the girlfriends' mothers. And they brought the boyfriends out, and they fought, right there on television. Toby, tell me: these people don't vote, do they?
   Aaron Sorkin, *The West Wing*, 2000

See also: CAMPAIGNING, DEMOCRACY, ELECTIONS, MAJORITY

W

#WALES AND THE WELSH

When all else fails
Try Wales.
  Christopher Logue, 1926–2011, poet, 'To a Friend in
  Search of Rural Seclusion'

... we can trace almost all the disasters of English history to
the influence of Wales.
  Evelyn Waugh, 1903–66, *Decline and Fall*, 1928

There are still parts of Wales where the only concession to
gaiety is a striped shroud.
  Gwyn Thomas, 1913–81, *Punch*, 1958

The Welsh are so damn Welsh that it looks like affectation.
  Sir Alexander Raleigh, 1861–1922, English critic and
  essayist

I'm used to being unpopular. I'm a Conservative and I'm
from Wales.
  Nigel Evans, Conservative politician

See also: BRITAIN AND THE BRITISH

#WAR

War does not determine who is right – only who is left.
  Anon.

War will exist as long as there's a food chain.
  P. J. O'Rourke, *Holidays in Hell*, 1989

I can understand why mankind hasn't given up war. During a war you get to drive tanks through the sides of buildings and shoot foreigners – two things that are usually frowned on during peacetime.
  P. J. O'Rourke, *Holidays in Hell*, 1989

War is nothing more than the continuation of politics by other means.
  Carl von Clausewitz, 1780–1831, Prussian soldier and military theorist

You can't say that civilisation don't advance, for in every war they kill you in a new way.
  Will Rogers, 1879–1935, American commentator and humorist

The belief in the possibility of a short, decisive war appears to be one of the most ancient and dangerous of human illusions.
  Robert Lynd, 1879–1949, Irish writer and nationalist

And the draft is white people sending black people to fight yellow people to protect the country they stole from red people.
  James Rado and Gerome Ragni, *Hair*, 1967

DRAFT BEER NOT STUDENTS!
  Vietnam War bumper sticker

Bombing can end the war! Bomb the Pentagon now!
  Vietnam War graffito

I'm fed up to the ears with old men dreaming up wars for
young men to die in.
  George McGovern, Senator and Democratic nominee in
  1972 US election

To destroy is still the strongest instinct of our nature.
  Max Beerbohm, 1872–1956, English essayist and novelist

Force, and fraud, are in war the two cardinal virtues.
  John Milton, 1608–74, English poet and polemicist

Battle, n. A method of untying with the teeth a political
knot that would not yield to the tongue.
  Ambrose Bierce, 1842–1913, *The Devil's Dictionary*, 1911

In time of war, the first casualty is truth.
  Boake Carter, 1903–44, American broadcast journalist
  (often misattributed to the Athenian tragedian Aeschylus,
  525–456 BC)

We are going to have peace even if we have to fight for it.
  Dwight D. Eisenhower, 1890–1969, 34th President of the
  United States, 1953–61

After each war there is a little less democracy to save.
  Brooks Atkinson, 1894–1984, *Once Around the Sun*, 1951

All wars are popular for the first thirty days.
   Arthur Schlesinger Jr, 1917–2007, American historian and
   social critic

They told me it would disrupt my life less if I got killed sooner.
   Joseph Heller, 1923–99, American novelist

Men love war because it allows them to look serious.
Because it is the one thing that stops women laughing
at them.
   John Fowles, 1926–2005, *The Magus*, 1965

But that was war. Just about all he could find in its favor
was that it paid well and liberated children from the perni-
cious influence of their parents.
   Joseph Heller, *Catch-22*, 1961

The grim fact is that we prepare for war like precocious
giants and for peace like retarded pygmies.
   Lester B. Pearson, 1897–1972, Canadian historian, diplomat and Prime Minister

At Victoria Station the RTO gave me a travel warrant, a
white feather and a picture of Hitler marked 'This is your
enemy'. I searched every compartment but he wasn't on
the train.
   Spike Milligan, 1918–2002, *Adolf Hitler: My Part in His
   Downfall*, 1971

Another such victory and we are ruined.
   Pyrrhus, 319–272 BC, Greek general and statesman

Very little is known about the war of 1812 because the
Americans lost it.

> Eric Nicol, 1919–2011, Canadian humorous columnist

Cluster bombs are perhaps not good in themselves, but
when they are dropped on identifiable concentrations of
Taliban troops, they do have a heartening effect.

> Christopher Hitchens, 1949–2011, British-American jour-
> nalist and controversialist

The object of war is not to die for your country but to make
the other bastard die for his.

> General George S. Patton, 1885–1945, served in the First
> and Second World Wars

How is the world ruled and led to war? Diplomats lie
to journalists and believe those lies when they see them
in print.

> Karl Kraus, 1874–1936, Austrian essayist and satirist,
> *Nachts*, 1918

A prisoner of war is a man who tries to kill you and fails,
and then asks you not to kill him.

> Winston Churchill, 1874–1965, quoted in *The Observer*,
> 1952

Nothing in life is so exhilarating as to be shot at without
result.

> Winston Churchill, *The Malakand Field Force*, 1898

History is littered with the wars which everybody knew
would never happen.

> Enoch Powell, 1912–98, Conservative politician, speech to
> Conservative Party Conference, 1967

I have never understood this liking for war. It panders to instincts already catered for within the scope of any respectable domestic establishment.
    Alan Bennett, *Forty Years On*, 1968

A general and a bit of shooting makes you forget your troubles ... it takes your mind off the cost of living.
    Brendan Behan, 1923–64, *The Hostage*, 1958

The quickest way of ending a war is to lose it.
    George Orwell, 1903–1950, 'Shooting an Elephant', 1950

As long as war is regarded as wicked, it will always have its fascination. When it is looked upon as vulgar it will cease to be popular.
    Oscar Wilde, 1854–1900, 'The Critic as Artist', 1890

Obama 'shocked and saddened'
    President Obama has described his shock after receiving news that a US soldier has gone rogue and killed a load of Afghan civilians.
    'The idea that a lone US gunman could kill all these innocent civilians instead of them being bombed by US drone attacks is appalling.
    'The last thing the US military want when they're indiscriminately killing civilians is to have their good name besmirched by a lone gunman indiscriminately killing Afghan civilians.'
    Private Eye, 2012

See also: THE ARMY, DEFENCE, ENEMIES, IRAQ WAR, THE MILITARY, NUCLEAR WEAPONS

#WAR ON TERROR

Terrorism is the tactic of demanding the impossible, and demanding it at gunpoint.
   Christopher Hitchens

... as frightening as terrorism is, it's the weapon of losers. The minute somebody sets off a suicide bomb, you can be sure that person doesn't have 'career prospects'. And no matter how horrendous a terrorist attack is, it's still conducted by losers. Winners don't need to hijack airplanes. Winners have an Air Force.
   P. J. O'Rourke, libertarian journalist and commentator, 2004

We've finally given liberals a war against fundamentalism, and they don't want to fight it. They would, except it would put them on the same side as the United States.
   Ann Coulter, American commentator and controversialist

In order to express their displeasure with the idea that Muslims are violent, thousands of Muslims around the world engaged in rioting, arson, mob savagery, flag-burning, murder and mayhem, among other peaceful acts of nonviolence.
   Ann Coulter, reflecting on the Muhammad cartoons
   controversy, 2006

Liberals hate America, they hate flag-wavers, they hate abortion opponents, they hate all religions except Islam, post 9/11. Even Islamic terrorists don't hate America like liberals do. They don't have the energy. If they had that much energy, they'd have indoor plumbing by now.
   Ann Coulter, *Slander*, 2002

President Bartlet: A martyr would rather suffer death at the hands of an oppressor than renounce his beliefs. Killing yourself and innocent people to make a point is sick, twisted, brutal, dumb-ass murder. And let me leave you with this thought ... we don't need martyrs right now. We need heroes. A hero would die for his country but he'd much rather live for it.

   Aaron Sorkin, *The West Wing*, 2001

Bitter after being snubbed for membership in the 'Axis of Evil', Libya, China, and Syria today announced they had formed the 'Axis of Just as Evil', which they said would be way eviller than that stupid Iran–Iraq–North Korea axis President Bush warned of in his State of the Union address.

   SatireWire, 2002

According to a new report from Afghanistan, the hottest music over there right now is disco. So, we've achieved a compromise here. We brought them out of the thirteenth century, but only took them up to 1978.

   Jay Leno

Today more al Qaeda and Taliban prisoners were flown to Guantanamo Bay in Cuba. On the plane they are bound, they are sedated, they are chained to their chairs. Or, as Continental calls it, coach.

   Jay Leno, 2002

Counter-terrorism experts say that Osama bin Laden may be hiding secret messages on pornographic websites. You know what that means, Clinton could find this guy before Bush.

   Jay Leno

Yasser Arafat died earlier this week in Paris. And in lieu of flowers, the Arafat family asked that everyone just throw rocks.

Jay Leno, 2004

CBS news anchor Dan Rather has interviewed Iraqi dictator Saddam Hussein. When asked what it was like to talk to a crazy man, Saddam said, 'It's not so bad.'

Conan O'Brien, late-night talk-show host, 2003

It's been reported that the FBI is visiting libraries nationwide and checking the reading records of people it finds suspicious. When asked about it, President Bush said, 'I've always been suspicious of people who go to libraries.'

Conan O'Brien, 2007

A new poll shows Americans have a more negative view of Muslims than they did back in 2002. That's because they never hear about any of the good bombings.

Jimmy Fallon, late-night talk-show host, 2009

I flew this past weekend. I went through airport security and said to the guy, 'Is everything okay?' He said, 'You might want to have that mole on your ass checked out.'

Jay Leno

On Friday, Umar Farouk Abdulmutallab, the Nigerian man who ignited his underpants in a failed attempt to blow up a jet landing in Detroit, pled not guilty to six federal charges, while his testicles pled guilty in absentia.

Seth Meyers, *Saturday Night Live*, 2011

Security here in New York City is still very tight. Hookers in Times Square now are demanding two forms of fake ID.
    David Letterman, late-night talk-show host

I think the next election just got a lot easier for President Obama 'cause his response to every question during the debates will be: 'Wait, I forget... Did you kill Osama bin Laden? Or did I kill Osama bin Laden? Oh no, it was me, wasn't it?'
    Craig Ferguson, late-night talk-show host, reacting to the
    assassination of Osama bin Laden, 2011

See also: OSAMA BIN LADEN, IRAQ WAR, MULTICULTURALISM

#WASHINGTON

I remember when I first came to Washington. For the first six months you wonder how the hell you ever got here. For the next six months you wonder how the hell the rest of them ever got here.
    Harry S. Truman, 1884–1972, 33rd President of the United
    States, 1945–53

The farther you get away from Washington, the more you think that things are under control there.
    Art Buchwald, 1925–2007, American humorous
    commentator

Washington is a pool of money surrounded by people who want some.
    David Brinkley, 1920–2003, television commentator

Washington is a city of southern efficiency and northern charm.

> John F. Kennedy, 1917–63, 35th President of the United States, 1961–63, quoted in Arthur M. Schlesinger Jr's *A Thousand Days*, 1965

If hypocrisy were gold, the Capitol would be Fort Knox.

> Senator John McCain, 1994

Things get very lonely in Washington sometimes. The real voice of the great people of America sometimes sounds faint and distant in that strange city. You hear politics until you wish that both parties were smothered in their own gas.

> Woodrow Wilson, 1856–1924, 28th President of the United States, 1913–21, speech, St Louis, Missouri, 1919

You want a friend in Washington? Get a dog.

> Harry S. Truman

Washington – Hubbub of the Universe.

> Anon., *Reader's Digest*

There's nothing so permanent as a temporary job in Washington.

> George Allen, Republican Senator

When I first went to Washington, I thought, what is l'il ole me doing with these ninety-nine great people? Now I ask myself, what am I doing with these ninety-nine jerks?

> S. I. Hayakawa, 1906–92, American academic and US Senator

I love to go to Washington – if only to be near my money.
    Bob Hope, 1903–2003, American comedian

I find in Washington that when you ask what time it is you get different answers from Democrats and Republicans; 435 answers from the House of Representatives; a 500-page report from some consultants on how to tell time; no answer from your lawyer and a bill for $ 1,000.
    R. Tim McNamar, Deputy Secretary of the Treasury under
    President Reagan

See also: GOVERNMENT

#WASHINGTON, GEORGE, 1732-99, FIRST PRESIDENT OF THE UNITED STATES, 1789-97

That George Washington was not a scholar is certain. That he is too illiterate, unlearned, unread for his station is equally beyond dispute.
    John Adams, 1735–1826, 2nd President of the United States,
    1797–1801, American Founding Father, lawyer, statesman
    and diplomat

... a sordid, ambitious, vain, proud, arrogant and vindictive knave.
    General Charles Lee, 1732–82, British soldier during the
    American War of Independence

See also: PRESIDENCY

#WEALTH

If you can count your money, you don't have a billion dollars.
  J. Paul Getty, 1892–1976, American industrialist and
  billionaire

If you pick up a starving dog and make him prosperous, he will not bite you. This is the principal difference between a man and a dog.
  Mark Twain, 1835–1910, American writer and humorist

Nothing is more admirable than the fortitude with which millionaires tolerate the disadvantages of their wealth.
  Rex Stout, 1886–1975, American writer of detective fiction

When a man tells you he got rich through hard work, ask him *whose*.
  Don Marquis, 1878–1937, American humorous poet and
  playwright

Some day I want to be rich. Some people get so rich they lose all respect for humanity. That's how rich I want to be.
  Rita Rudner, American comedian

See also: BANKS AND BANKING, BIG BUSINESS, BUSINESS, CAPITALISM, CREDIT CRUNCH, ECONOMICS AND ECONOMISTS, ECONOMY, INFLATION, MONEY, POVERTY, RICH AND POOR, STOCK MARKET AND WALL STREET, TAXATION

#WHITE HOUSE, THE

The White House is the finest jail in the world.
  Harry S. Truman

I don't know whether it's the finest public housing in America or the crown jewel of the American penal system.
  Bill Clinton, 42nd President of the United States, 1993–2001

Leo [signing Christmas cards]: Who the hell is this guy and why would I care if he has a merry Christmas?
Margaret: Just sign the damn thing.
  Aaron Sorkin and Rick Cleveland, *The West Wing*, 1999

C. J.: They sent me two turkeys. The most photo-friendly of the two gets a Presidential pardon and a full life at a children's zoo. The runner-up gets eaten.
President Bartlet: If the Oscars were like that, I'd watch.
  Aaron Sorkin, *The West Wing*,

Charlie: You send a Christmas card to everyone who writes a letter to the White House.
President Bartlet: I do?
Charlie: Yes, sir. And somewhere around a million people wrote you letters this year.
Bartlet: Okay, but some of those were death threats.
Charlie: They've weeded those out.
  Aaron Sorkin, *The West Wing*,

See also: PRESIDENCY, WASHINGTON

#WILSON, HAROLD, LABOUR PRIME MINISTER, 1964–70, 1974–76

The only reason Harold Wilson as a child had to go to school without boots on, was that his boots were probably too small for him.

> Harold Macmillan, 1894–1986, Conservative Prime
> Minister, 1957–63 (attrib.)

See also: LABOUR PARTY, SOCIALISM

#WILSON, WOODROW, 1856–1924, 28TH PRESIDENT OF THE UNITED STATES, 1913–21

Mr Wilson's name among the Allies is like that of the rich uncle, and they have accepted his manners out of respect for his means.

> *Morning Post*, London, 1919

The spacious philanthropy which he exhaled upon Europe stopped quite sharply at the coasts of his own country.

> Winston Churchill, *The World Crisis*, 1929

Mr Wilson's mind, as has been the custom, will be closed all day Sunday.

> George S. Kaufman, 1889–1961, American playwright

I feel certain that Woodrow Wilson would not recognise a generous impulse if he met it on the street.

> William Howard Taft, 1857–1930, 27th President of the
> United States, 1909–13

He had to hold the reins and do the driving alone; it was the only kind of leadership he knew.

  Arthur S. Link, 1920–98, *Wilson: The Road to the White House*, 1947

Mr Wilson bores me with his fourteen points; why, God Almighty has only ten.

  Georges Clemenceau, 1841–1929, French statesman and journalist

See also: PRESIDENCY

#WORK

All professions are conspiracies against the laity.

  George Bernard Shaw, 1856–1950, *The Doctor's Dilemma*, 1911

Work is the curse of the drinking classes.

  Oscar Wilde

Work expands so as to fill the time available for its completion.

  C. Northcote Parkinson, 1909–93, *Parkinson's Law*, 1958

People who work sitting down get paid more than people who work standing up.

  Ogden Nash, 1902–71, American poet

The longer the title, the less important the job.

  George McGovern

If you don't like your job, you don't strike! You just go in every day, and do it really half-assed. That's the American way.

Homer Simpson, *The Simpsons*

See also: TRADES UNIONS